A WELLIE FULL
OF WATER

A WELLIE FULL OF WATER

CHRIS SANDFORD

AN ANGLER'S MIXED BAG OF
TRAVEL, TACKLE & TALL TALES

MEDLAR PRESS
2008

Published by the Medlar Press Limited,
The Grange, Ellesmere, Shropshire.
www.medlarpress.com

ISBN 978-1-899600-78-6

Produced in England by the Medlar Press Limited, Ellesmere.
Designed and typeset in 11 on 11^1/$_2$pt Bembo by Jonathan Ward-Allen.

Contents

Publisher's note

I'm never quite sure why publishers add little bits of text to the front of a book. Maybe it's to explain something about the content, though if you've got past the title of this little tome and failed to spot that it is, shall we say, a little on the lighter side of angling, then perhaps you shouldn't be reading it at all. Or perhaps you should, with a doctor's prescription.

Often the publisher adds a little about the writer's character or prowess in his or her chosen field. You know the sort of thing - his secret army career as the only trained boy actor to rise to the rank of Field Marshall by the age of seven (Damn. Sorry, Chris, it's out of the bag now). Or the time he hopped from Catterick to Bude for charity, using a Hardy tope rod to beat off the well wishers on his arrival. What I can do is take this opportunity to thank Chris for his support over the years for our magazine *Waterlog*. It's a magazine that people said would never last, but here we are, twelve years after it began, still going strong, and not least because of people like Chris. He didn't have to write for *Waterlog* but he did because he liked it. I think he identified with its eccentricity, but perhaps he was just being kind.

Anyway, the last thing Chris Sandford needs is a big bluff northerner like me lobbing platitudes in his direction about the qualities of his character or his book. He has earned the credit for this little masterpiece all by himself, by sheer hard work, lots of claret and above all, a sense of fun. *A Wellie Full of Water* meanders like a little stream with delights round every bend. I went round the bend myself, just retouching some of the photos . . .

JWA

Foreword

Many of us have photos of ourselves with a memorable fish but I don't know of any other angler apart from Chris Sandford who has a photo on his loo wall of his younger self singing with the Beatles.

Of course, that claim to fame doesn't necessarily make him a more accomplished fisher but it does perhaps hint at a breadth of skills and interests.

I have known Chris for over twenty years and am happy to say that on occasions in his role as producer and writer of radio commercials he employed me, which is how we met, so I probably owe him these few words.

We both started fishing seriously only in our later years and at about the same time, he for carp, I for trout, but whereas I limit myself pretty much to salmon in Scotland and trout in southern rivers, Chris now seems to follow in Negley Farson's footsteps and fishes worldwide for anything with fins.

The son of a comic and no mean 'turn' himself, his *A Wellie Full of Water* is an entertaining collection of tales resulting from his visits to vintage tackle shows, game fairs, fly tying events and riverbanks far flung and sometimes far fetched. To me the most attractive ingredient in the book is his delightful wife but that's another story

A really most enjoyable bedside read.

Geoffrey Palmer

A Wellie Full of Water is a mixed bag of travel, tackle and tall tales taken from ten years of my Waterlog articles. So whether you find yourself bedside, bankside or bogside, dip in when the mood takes you and enjoy!

When I started to list all those I should thank for their input it became clear that there was no 'top of the bill' so at a press of a computer key my thanks go alphabetically to:

Allcock & Co.; whose wonderful old tackle is the mainstay of my vintage collection.

David Beazley; whose encyclopaedic knowledge of angling art and literature has come to my rescue more times than I can count, and to whom I dedicate the chapter 'Fred G. Shad's *Concise Treatise*'!

Mark Bowler; Editor of *Fly Fishing and Fly Tying* who is always open to new ideas and encourages me to 'go for it' in my monthly column.

JJ Cale; for being such a great influence on Eric Clapton!

Peter Cockwill; who got me started on the fly rod, gave me fly-tying lessons (see 'I'll Never Do It') and arranged some of the more exotic locations for my TV series *Just Fishin'*.

Peter Drennan; whose wit and wisdom is as durable as his excellent fishing tackle.

Iain Dunne; who worked with me for many years at my production company Hobo Radio. He taught me how to be patient and how to fit some of the world's greatest advertising ideas into thirty seconds.

Robin Elwes; who allows me to fish his stretch of the river Test, and many years ago had the unenviable task of teaching me to cast a salmon line.

Fish; for being there!

Terry Griffiths; whose photographic skills are demonstrated throughout my first book *The Best of British Baits* and who has allowed me to use many of his images from my archive in the pages that follow.

John Hotchkiss; who, as UK producer for the TV series *The Take*, employed me as its voice-over, and has subsequently invited me for far too many wonderful days on the river Itchen.

Bob James; who introduced me to the Hampshire Avon, secret French carp lakes and Hugh Miles.

Genghis Khan; who stopped me veering too far to the right!

John Knott; whose knowledge of angling history, especially that of fly fishing, has been invaluable - not only when researching material for an article, but also when he has accompanied me on trips with my Vintage Fishing Tackle Road Show, which raises money for SPARKS (Sport Aiding Medical Research for Kids)

Geoffrey Palmer; who has kindly written the foreword for this collection of ramblings and has my sincere thanks for constantly inviting my wife and I to fish on some of the country's best salmon rivers.

Gelly Sandford; who changed my life and has become far too skilled with a fishing rod, as with everything else she decides to master!

Steve Thornton; who brought his cameras when my wife and I fished the Lozère region of France. See 'Me and the Mrs…Fishes - France', where his

skills speak for themselves!

Max Wall; for making me laugh.

Ricky Walker; who produced and directed my TV series *Just Fishin'*. We had the best of times and he taught me it was quite possible to make five hours of television without a script! "Just make it up as you go along, Chris!" which is Scottish for, "Stand there and do as you're told!"

Jon Ward-Allen; for having the patience to put this compendium together so skilfully!

Zen; for giving us something to talk about in the Sixties!

Zorba the Greek; for filling up this awkward little space at the end of the column to make the page balance.

For my son Jamie and for his children…
as soon as they appear!

I took a walk,
I took a rod,
I saw a fish and caught her.
I turned for home
And missed the path.
A wellie full of water!

Me and the Mrs … Fishes ! - France

On 22nd September, 1878, Robert Louis Stevenson spent twelve days with a donkey called Modestine walking the 220 kilometres from Le Monestier-sur-Gazeille in the north of the French Lozère region, to St-Jean-du-Gard in the south.

On 19th July, 2005, my journey to this beautiful part of France started from Stansted airport with a more conventional companion . . . my wife, Gelly!

Ryanair run a very efficient, low cost service to Rodez, but be warned, they only allow you 15kg of luggage each. Our two hold-alls cost us over £30 extra, each way!

We'd visited the Lozère region a couple of years ago, but never seriously considered the fishing. Lying in the south-east of France, this region encompasses half a million hectares of stunningly beautiful National Heritage countryside, including 2,700 kilometres of Category 1 trout rivers and streams.

These 'rod quivering' facts had been pointed out to me by Akadi de Rakoff, who acts as a most genial 'Mr Fixit' for those who wish to wet a line almost anywhere in France. Depending on your needs, he will recommend locations, guides and accommodation, which can be anything from a family gîte to a five-star chateau. He suggested that to get a 'feel' for the region, a whistle-stop tour, fishing with three local guides over four days, would do the trick.

Our first evening was spent on the banks of the Treyere river with English-speaking guide Arnaud Pellegrin. He examined our equipment and clothing, nodding with satisfaction, until he came to the join between my line and tippet.

"I do not like zis mettod," he said, "Eet could be sticking in zee top ring and you could be 'aving zee snap off!"

"Right then," I said, visualising huge fish diving suddenly and hooping the rod over. My line to tippet join has never failed me yet; it is constructed by using the well-known method of exposing the

inner core of the line and whipping a loop, so that one can make a 'loop to loop' join with the tippet material. I promised to change it the very next day if I lost a fish.

As we sat waiting for the evening rise, Arnaud tied us some simple sedge patterns and assured us that this was the only fly we would need. He was right. Gelly was more than happy to catch some of the smallest trout we have ever seen, and I was happy to sit on the bank and watch the sunset. The cool of the evening was most welcome, as daytime temperatures were building to a record high.

Accommodation, though functional, was not the high point of our trip.

However, the first night in Relais du Saint-Roch in Saint Alban sur Limagnole, was the exception. We were greeted by our host, Christian Chavignon, who made us most welcome and cooked us a delicious selection of local dishes. The hotel is part of the Demures de Lozère group, which boasts nine fine hotels across the region. The other accommodation recommended by the Tourist Board, was at best, adequate and at worst, down right spartan!

The next day, the temperature soared into the eighties and although we looked at a few rivers and had a half-hearted 'dabble', we soon decided to move on to meet Stephane Faudon and fish the river

Lot near Florac. Stephane falls into the 'very chummy' category of fishing guides. Although he had two other clients with him that day, he did his best to split his time between the four of us. At lunchtime he energetically produced table, chairs and a splendid spread from the back of his customised fishing van.

Once again, small sedge patterns produced small fish, though I'm sure there were bigger fish to be caught, had we had more time.

Our final day was without doubt, our most adventurous. Serge Rollo is a local guide but clients all over the world have enjoyed his skills. His years in Montana guiding French anglers have given him a

good knowledge of English, and he has that indefinable quality which more than assures you that you are in capable hands.

He drove us, for an hour-and-a-half, high into the mountains past the tiny village of Le Pont de Montvert and through some of the Lozère's most breathtaking scenery. When we eventually stopped at about 1,600 metres, Serge explained that we should change into our waders and boots because "We must now take a petite promenade." I don't know about you, but a half-hour walk in waders in what must have been at least eighty-five degrees of heat is not my idea of 'fun' . . . but it was worth it!

The boulder-strewn reaches at the source of the Tarn are a fly fisherman's

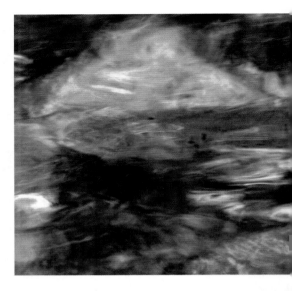

paradise. I spent the first half-hour sitting in the river trying to get my temperature back to normal whilst Gelly and Serge vanished downstream. The fishing was very relaxed; I crept around huge boulders and almost dapped tiny size 20 midges to some of the most obliging 5- and 6-inch browns. It's the sort of fishing, that when you recall the memory, you always smile.

I'd just decided to rest in the shade, when a call from Gelly sent me careering down the river and, there it was . . . the biggest fish of the trip. Not a monster, but big enough. Serge got a kiss, and I got to carry Gelly's rod back to the car!

We were so hot and tired when we got there that I truly thought this was the end of our Lozère fishing, but Serge still had one more trick up his sleeve, "You like to catch some barbel on the fly?" he said.

We sped back down the mountain collecting cold drinks, local cherries and ice creams along the way, arriving at the spectacular Gorge du Tarn near St Enimie around teatime.

Wading out into the shallows, Serge pointed out three barbel that were 'hoovering' up all manner of tasty morsels. One step too close and they vanished. But then came the moment that guaranteed that we were unlikely to connect with any of these spooky bottom-feeders. Around the corner of this shallow, gin clear river came a boatload of waving pensioners! What can you do? You wave back and smile hoping that

this is a rare occurrence. When the second boat passed, I noticed a distinct change of attitude in the passengers. They were still friendly, but there was a definite sense of 'Ooh la la' among the male contingent. Looking over my shoulder, all became clear. Mrs Sandford had had quite enough of feeling too hot and was wearing a baseball cap, a short waistcoat, a very small bathing costume and wading boots! We didn't catch a barbel but Gelly, having engaged her audience, was casting better than ever!

On our way home, I was reading through the tourist literature when I came across a leaflet dedicated entirely to Robert Louis Stevenson's walk. Today you can follow in his footsteps in easy stages and have your luggage moved to the next hotel down the trail so that your stroll is unencumbered. The trail passes some fine fishing. So, if you're a hiker and a fisher . . . what are you waiting for?

If you really want to make the experience even more authentic, there are no less than three companies who will hire you a donkey. Just make sure they don't charge you excess baggage!

The Art of Crossdressing

A 'crosswind' is not as one might think, an angry angler, neither does it have anything to do with the elements. It is in fact a type of threadline or fixed-spool reel with a tilting spool which lays the line across itself to eliminate 'bedding in'. Patented by Percy W. Felton in May 1935 it was an immediate success and could be purchased from Allcock & Co with half bale-arm or finger pick-up.

In 1936 Felton sealed the reel's reputation by winning four major prizes in the Crystal Palace Casting Championships.

Richard Walker used the reel in his early carp-fishing days and so impressed was E. Marshall Hardy with the new invention that he interviewed Felton for his book *Angling Ways*. In the chapter 'Coarse Fish and the Threadline' Felton tells us how he came upon the idea: "My wife and I used to quite often take our supper with us and spend the early summer evenings on the beach. I didn't take a rod, but eventually I thought it might be worth while if I had the means of increasing my casting powers. I set out to arrange matters so that, first, the line would not snatch as the spool was emptied. The need for each coil of line to lie at an angle to its neighbours, being thus prevented from becoming pinched between any underlying coils, gave birth to the criss cross idea which was subsequently developed so that each coil traversed the full width of the drum. My wife, who does not fish, was using a ball of crochet cotton when these thoughts were being considered, and this crystallised my aim to invent a fixed-spool reel based on the principles I have stated.

And the rest as they say is history . . . but not quite!

It seems that as soon as there is a successful innovation on the market someone somewhere has to bastardise it. In this case it was the very company who had developed the Crosswind with Felton Allcock & Co!

The OTO is a Crosswinding Sidecaster which they developed for the French market. Never has there been a clumsier

or more unwieldy piece of angling equipment. Mind you, it is the only one I have ever seen, and you couldn't wrest it from my grasp unless you could find me something even sillier. Come to think of it, I wouldn't mind having a 'one to one' with old Felton and asking him what he thought of the OTO but I'm sure the operator would say, "Could you hold the line Sir, he's still spinning in his grave!"

John Ploughshears

1902-1993

Old John Ploughshears is dead now. He died suddenly at the grand old age of ninety-one in the autumn of 1993. He was one of the least known, but undoubtedly, one of the finest cane-rod builders the world has ever seen.

When I met him in the early Eighties, he was still building the occasional rod for 'special' customers, but most of his days were spent overseeing his furniture-building business and caravanning with his wife Vera.

I asked him if he would build me a Mk IV. He said, "I might . . . I s'pose you'll be fishing for them soppy old carps?" I admitted that I probably would and he smiled and shook his head. "Ah well," he said, "each to their own . . . "

He finally agreed to build me a rod and suggested that I contact him again eighteen months later. "Will you sign it?" I asked. "No son," he said, "I don't sign

'em. Can't stand all that showin' off! I puts me initials under the whips near the butt ring. But don't you worry, you'll know it's mine!"

Before I left, I took a moment to admire some of the old photographs that stood in 'pride of place' on his mantelpiece: famous anglers, rod in hand, smiling at the camera, groups of fishermen posing outside their club headquarters, a golden retriever sitting next to a huge salmon. But, there was one shot that intrigued me - it showed a group of men posing rather like a football team. They each held a two-piece rod in front of them but they were all blindfolded! "What's the story behind that photograph?" I asked. "Ah . . . " said John, "it's a long'n. I'll tell you all about that when you collect your rod."

The months dragged past, but eighteen months later, almost to the day, I received a card, which in John's spidery hand, read: 'Mk IV ready, please collect Saturday noon from works. JP'

John's house was down a narrow lane, with his works a quarter of a mile further on. He greeted me with a smile and suggested I might enjoy 'the five dollar tour' of his furniture business. We passed through the carpentry workshops and entered what can only be described as, an immense shed. There was a strong smell of varnish. Down the centre of this area, there were three huge vats with a gantry supporting three platforms that extended out over the vats. John explained, "An individual item of furniture is taken up on the hoist and guided in by the Dipper. Each of the three vats contains a different shade: light, medium and dark. After dippin', each item is then swung back to the dripping tray where it's finished off by the Brusher. All the varnishes are based on the 'Mellow Glow' formula I use on me rods."

I asked John if he would pass the formula on. "No," he said, "I still mix it up meself . . . I've no one to leave it to, so when I go . . . it's done."

There was a quiet moment as he looked up at the gantry and along at the vats. Then, turning to me he said, "Righto, son. Let's sort out this rod of yours."

Back at the house, Vera had made a pot of tea. John went to the corner cupboard in the living room, took out the Mk IV and, looking over his glasses, said, "There you are then, what do you think of that?"

I was speechless. There it was, the dark cane, the 'Mellow Glow' finish and the dark green whips. Finally, I managed to say, "What do I owe you John?" "Well," he said, "here's the deal . . . if you promise to use it, and not stick it up on the wall with all them others you've got . . . it's yours!"

Even now as I recall that wonderful day, there's a lump in my throat, and there most certainly was then. So much so that I almost forgot to ask about the photograph of the blind-folded chaps holding the rods.

"Have another cuppa tea," said John, "and I'll tell you a story.

"It all started in a black-out in the Second War. We were workin' late 'cos we 'ad to get a dozen rods out on a special order. There was only three of us - me, Tom and old Jed. There should have been eight, but all the others 'ad been called up and were Gawd knows where. Anyway, we knew old Jed's eyesight weren't too good but we never realised that 'e 'ardly looked at the rod when 'e was whippin' up. So, this particular teatime, all the lights went out, and I'm cursing and sayin' we'll 'ave to stop, when old Jed pipes up and says that it don't bother 'im, and carries on whippin' . . . so, me and Tom looks at each other and tries to give it a go without lookin!

"Well, after a bit, we got the 'ang of it and in the weeks and months to come, perfected the art, if you like! Only two of the others come back from the war, but they thought it a bit of a challenge and 'ad a go as well! I forget who come up with the idea of an annual competition. Don't matter really, we all knew old Jed would win, even though 'e could 'ardly see a thing by then! The prize was a bottle of whisky and when we 'anded it over to Jed 'is old dog would go mad barking and 'e'd always say, 'Surely, it's someone else's turn?' Well, it never was, 'cos 'e was the best in the game, bless 'im. They're all gone now . . . that snap is all that's left."

I thanked him again and tried to pay him something for the rod. "No, no," he said, "you go and catch a few bigguns and that will be reward enough for me!"

I never saw John Ploughshears again, but I got a call from Vera to tell me of his sad passing in September of 1993.

The funeral was held in the little church not half a mile from John's works, so I expect he's still keeping a eye on things.

As we left the church and went to look at the flowers that had been sent from all over the world, Vera confided in me. She said, "I've kept a bit quiet about how he died but I want to tell you." She smiled and looked down at the flowers. "God bless him," she said, "but he was an obstinate man. I tried to persuade him to let one of the men do it, but he wouldn't listen. You see, he'd always mix the varnish for the vats himself, then he'd go up on the gantry and watch it pumped in. I told him to be careful, but he always used to say 'stop fussin'. He'd just finished watching the medium vat fill up, when he slipped and fell. Nothing anyone could do . . . he'd never learnt to swim, so that was that." Vera lifted her glasses and wiped away a tear. "Still," she said, "I suppose that's how he'd have wanted it . . . he had a horrible death, but a lovely finish!"

Mr Cook's Gaff

There is usually a story behind every piece of unusual fishing tackle, but in the case of this spring-loaded automatic gaff I have yet to hear a murmur of explanation. My theory however, based on not one jot of evidence, is that in the early months of 1891 Mr F. Cook had a bad day. Having hooked a large fish and brought it to the bank he leaned forward to gaff it, and it escaped. Returning home and proceeding to his workshop in his garden shed, he turned dramatically at the back door, fixed his wife with a martyred gaze and exclaimed "Don't wait up . . . I may be some time." Three days later he emerged triumphant clutching a set of patent drawings which were registered and then eventually granted patent number 5491 on 28th March, 1891.

More at home in a medieval torture chamber than on a riverbank, the 'Cook's Gaff' is a fiendish apparatus. The sprung hooks are primed by sliding the cocking sleeve towards the handle. The angler then approaches his quarry, holds the device over the fish's head, and presses the trigger causing the hooks to snap shut. Not surprisingly the 'Cook's Gaff' is a rare collector's item and what truly inspired its creation we may never know. Until we do I'm sticking to my theory!

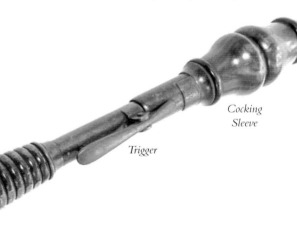

Cocking Sleeve

Trigger

Mr Cook's Gaff

Teach Your Children Well

The day after I returned from Italy last July, my wife announced that, for my birthday, she had managed to book seats that evening at the Hammersmith Apollo to see Crosby, Stills and Nash on the final night of their UK tour. I've known Graham Nash since the Sixties so, apart from renewing our friendship, I was interested to discover how the band would sound in 2005.

It was an extraordinary evening; they sounded better than ever and spent two hours laying down the 'good stuff' that, as they say in all the pop biographies, 'defined a generation'. The final song of the evening was Graham's composition, 'Teach Your Children Well' and, for a moment, I was sitting there in my flared velvet jeans, tribal beads and rather more hair than I have now. It struck me that the lyrics are just as poignant today as they were all those years ago. But as I listened, the picture that came to mind was not inspired by Woodstock or any image connected with the 'Flower Power' generation. It was of a field I had

visited only days earlier on the outskirts of the village of Castel di Sangro in a mountainous Italian region two hours south-east of Rome.

As guests of the SIM Fly Festival (School Italian Mosca), my wife and I were taken on a tour of points of interest, and the field was the first stop. It was an amazing sight. At least a hundred and fifty men and women of all ages were learning to fly cast. A team of qualified instructors busied around their small groups of charges and there were never less than a hundred fly lines in the air at any given moment. The most interesting group for me was in the far corner of the field. Half a dozen children aged between nine and fifteen were happily being put through their paces by a patient and cheerful instructress. When they weren't casting they were scrabbling about, collecting all manner of bugs and grubs which they brought to her for approval and identification. She was indeed, 'Teaching her Children Well'!

The fly-fishing festival offers an opportunity for anyone in Italy, regardless of their social standing, to learn more about the art of fly fishing. The three day festival is funded by the government, along with the local council and some commercial businesses. It is run from a museum which occupies a converted monastery on the outskirts of the town. The building also houses an angling museum that provided a cool haven as the temperature soared into the 90s.

British angling interests were well represented. Robin Armstrong brought a small exhibition of his much sought after art which was so highly regarded by the organisers that they reproduced one painting on the label of the festival wine! Steve Thornton continued to amaze onlookers by tying a range of truly outstanding bugs and Charles Jardine not only demonstrated his painting skills but when Sky TV arrived, he almost emptied the river of small trout with a team of Czech Nymphs. A few of the Italian fishers were sadly lacking in 'waterside etiquette', and the third time a particularly insistent angler cast across Charles' line, causing the inevitable tangle, Charles smiled sweetly as only he can, cut off the fly and allowed the offending line to drift back to its owner!

The history of fly fishing was a major feature of the festival. The permanent exhibits in the museum encouraged collectors from all over Italy to display some of the rarest pieces in their collections. Enthusiasm is always the driving force behind any event of this kind and, without doubt, Giorgio Cavatorti must take the credit for not only establishing the museum but encouraging collectors to make this annual pilgrimage.

Giorgio has written three books on the history of Italian angling and is a regular contributor to Italy's most prestigious fly fishing magazine: *Fly Line*.

Although my understanding of Italian doesn't reach far beyond the menu in our local restaurant, an article in a back issue of *Fly Line* caught my eye. And, as we sat in the cool of the monastery cloisters, I asked Giorgio to tell me the story of Saint Zeno:

"It was very exciting," he said . . . *"seven years ago, they were cleaning a painting in the small church of Borso Del Grappa (circa sixth century) about one hour North of Verona. It was a big picture, about 3 x 6 metres, but very difficult to access because it was behind the altar and the organ. But with the help of the local priest and a 5-metre ladder, the cleaning began. Soon it became clear that what had been thought to be Zeno's staff was in fact, a fly-fishing rod! Hanging from his rod were three flies and a grayling! The rod is about eight foot long, similar to our modern rods and it was interesting to note that the rod and flies are in the foreground, and the holy book is in the background. The little finger of the Saint holds a loop of line to not only get the flies*

nearer to the observers' eyes, but to contrast them against the fabric of his robe.

"Saint Zeno died in ad 372 and this picture was painted by Jacobo Da Bassano in 1538. Saint Zenone (or Zeno as he is known today), was the eighth Bishop of Verona from ad 362 until his death. Tradition has it that he was African with a dark skin, as he is represented in the painted marble statue in the Basilica in Verona. He is the patron saint of fresh water fishers and in a church in Verona, there is a big stone on which, it is said, he used to sit and fish. The Latin inscription on the stone reads as follows:

' . . . Hoc super incumbens saxo
Probe fluminis undam
Zeno pater tremula
Captabat arundine pisces'

(sitting on this stone, near the wave of the river, Father Zenone used to fish with his flexible rod).

" . . . obviously, as an angling historian I was excited to think that we could place this most ancient evidence regarding fly fishing in Italy. In the UK you are quite rightly proud of your Treatyse of Fyshinge Wyth an Angle by Dame Juliana Berners (1496) and we know that even before Zeno and Berners, the earliest known book of fly fishing and dressing was written by Eliano (ad 175-235) and reported on the fly fishing in Macedonia.

"I'm glad to tell you this story as it's important that we all share our fly fishing history. I'm sure Saint Zeno would approve . . . I hope he is smiling on us today!"

I'm sure he was. The whole atmosphere of the festival was quite special.

As I finish writing this article in late July, I'm listening to Crosby, Stills and Nash singing, 'Teach Your Children Well' once again. Perhaps we should all consider whether or not we know a child or teenager who might benefit from a few fly-casting lessons. Like the song says: 'Feed them on your dreams'!

"Sadly not, Sir!"

'A face like a smacked arse' is how my grandfather would have described the features of the man who walked into the Vintage Fishing Tackle Road Show tent at Chatsworth Angling Fair. It was getting towards going home time on the Sunday afternoon and it had been raining for two hours. The gentleman fixed me with a lazer-like stare, rummaged deep in his Barbour, which frankly could have done with an oil change, and produced a very sad-looking fixed-spool reel. Crashing it down on one of our glass-topped cabinets, he stood back and said "Whaddya think of that then?"

"Well," I offered, "it might benefit from a bale-arm."

"No problem," said the man, "you can get spares, can't you? It's the first model you know!"

"Sadly not, Sir." I replied, and proceeded to explain that the first Mitchell only had the name on the side, not the numbers, and had a half bale-arm and a small knurled knob for turning the check on and off. His model, announced through scabs of encrusted groundbait, that it was a 300 and the little 'butterfly' check control told the rest of the story.

"Value?" he snapped.

"About a fiver for spares." He made a sort of snorting noise, said, "Please yourself," and snatching up his reel marched out of the tent. My wife Gelly sighed and muttered, "Elvis has left the building," and we all had another cup of tea!

CARPANO & PONS, and PONS, C. Aug.
3, 1948, Nos. 20530/48 and 20116/49. [Class
48] [Also in Group XXIV]

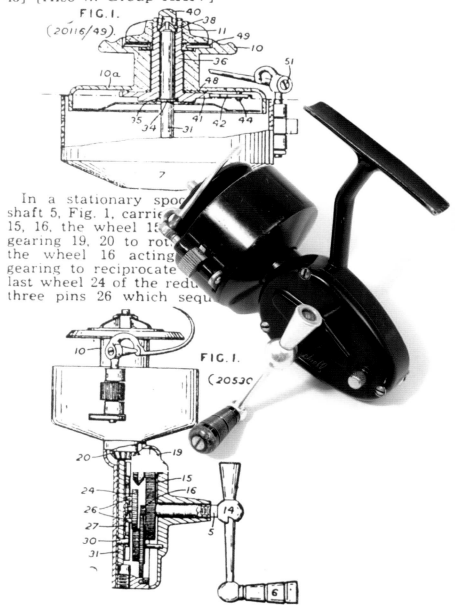

FIG. 1.
(20116/49).

In a stationary spo○○
shaft 5, Fig. 1, carrie○
15, 16, the wheel 1○
gearing 19, 20 to rot○
the wheel 16 acting
gearing to reciprocate
last wheel 24 of the redu○
three pins 26 which sequ○

FIG. 1.
(20530

I Like Geoffrey Palmer

I've known him for over twenty-five years, he's one of the UK's finest character actors, he's cheered up our TV screens with his performances in *Butterflies* and *As Time Goes By*, and his supporting roles in countless movies are always a treat. He's king of laconic delivery, an avid game fisher and, to coin an old-fashioned phrase, a jolly nice chap!

When I decided to add the fly rod to my angling armoury, he showed immense patience. I turned up for a day with him on the Test and, knowing I was still trying to master the fly cast, he asked to see how I was progressing. After watching me flail from side to side for a few moments, he muttered, "Well you seem to be able to cast sideways, perhaps you'd like to go over to that carrier and try something a little more conventional!"

When I thought I was competent enough to be seen on his local river Lodden, I bought a day with him in a charity auction. The weather and the setting were perfect. I wandered off downstream, while Geoffrey took the higher beat. I'd seen no sign of a fish until the river angled away for a few yards into a tunnel of Hawthorn. There, as the river turned almost at right-angles, a huge fish was sipping insects from the surface. There was no room to stand, so I crawled into the bushes, sat on the flap of my shoulder bag and flicked a tiny Hare's Ear on three feet of leader towards the fish. Suddenly a voice behind me said, "Christopher . . . we don't sit down when we're fly fishing!" Since that time, I have knelt occasionally, but whenever I've been tempted to sit, Geoffrey's words come back to haunt me.

Last year, my wife and I joined the 'Palmer Clan' on the Tweed. His expeditions to Scotland have become family outings. Son Charlie and daughter Harriet are both proficient salmon fishers, while his wife Sally, a talented artist, spends her time immortalising some of the more picturesque locations.

I've only fished for Atlantic salmon a few times in my chequered angling career and, as if it were pre-ordained, I've been met every time with the dreaded 'low water' . . . "You should have been here last week Sir, we were walking across their backs . . ." And of course as

soon as I leave, anglers have to wear special trusses so as not to rupture themselves dragging gargantuan fish on to the bank!

The year 2003 was a record year for the Tweed but, in spite of that, the Sandford 'Low Water Curse' took full effect for our two-day visit. I was convinced that Geoffrey now realised that to invite me anywhere near a salmon river would have the effect of most of the water draining back into the sea! So I was pleasantly surprised in early May of this year when he invited me for three days on the Lower Oykel.

I'd never seen this legendary Sutherland river, let alone fished it. "Just fly up to Inverness," he said, "hire a car, and you'll be at the Oykel Bridge Hotel in about one and a half hours. They've been having a terrific spring run, so it's all looking rather good."

We arrived at the hotel within half an hour of each other and went immediately to the riverbank to pursue the traditional practice of looking at the gauges. There wasn't enough water to wet their lowest extremities, let alone give an optimistic reading! So we took the only advisable action in these circumstances and had a nice cup of tea! We all agreed that the hotel was terrific . . . comfy beds, loads of

hot water and great food . . . and the company, even better.

The upside, as far as I was concerned, was that even with low water, once allotted my beat on this remote river, I could practice my Spey casting without causing too much hilarity among the locals!

The Oykel is the most beautiful of rivers, and although nothing was caught for the first two days, it was a privilege just to be there and walk the banks. On the evening of the second day, the forecast promised rain which duly arrived and continued for most of the night. Breakfast on my last day was a very optimistic affair – even the ghillies were smiling. When we met at the lunch hut it was a different story. One of our party thought he had seen a fish but wasn't sure, and that was about it.

After lunch, everyone swapped beats and I was left looking at an exquisite stretch of river that had been fished hard all morning by the rest of the group. I sat and looked at it for half an hour, then it struck me. The water was ten feet deep and the other anglers had fished floating lines with their flies going no deeper than about two feet. I rigged my 9-foot 9-weight trout rod with a clear intermediate line and on the second cast managed to hook a salmon. George, the head ghillie, arrived in the nick of time and estimated the fish at eight or nine pounds. Geoffrey also caught a fish of about the same weight, so that evening there was cause for great celebration!

It had been suggested to me that when dining at the Oykel Bridge Hotel, one was expected to wear a jacket and tie. I don't mind fancy dress occasionally and had packed my most tasteless fish tie for the last night. I arrived in the bar to spasmodic applause. The barman reached behind the bar, smiled and produced exactly the same tie! I congratulated him on his good taste and joined the rest of the party. What I didn't know was that he later sneaked the tie to Geoffrey who arrived wearing it and a deadpan expression, a few moments later!

I like Geoffrey Palmer!

Oh Trossachs!

The pike fly is the only imitation bait with a built-in casting aid. Drop the rod too far past your shoulder, and the fly smacks you in the back of the head with monotonous regularity. As fur and feathers take on water the danger increases. It's amazing how quickly one learns!

But I do like a challenge so, before setting off on my first serious attempt to catch a pike on the fly, I thought it best to try and glean a few tips from our angling ancestors. In *The Driffield Angler,* published around 1806, Alexander Mackintosh advises us that the fly should be '. . . about the thickness of a tomtit and about three inches long'. This is confirmed by Francis Francis in the third edition of his *Book of Angling* in 1872. He reports that the body of the fly is '. . . as thick as a man's little finger' and that '. . . this apparatus, more like a good size humming bird than anything else, is cast and worked like a salmon fly, and when pike are inclined to take it, it is the most sporting and agreeable way of fishing for them.'

A. J. Lane, in his diary, circa 1843, notes that in Irish lakes pike are fished for '. . . with a boat and four or five rods with flies on different lengths of line and then rowed very gently over the lake'. In 1847 Ephemera whets the appetite further in his *Hand Book of Angling* with the following passage '. . . in the latter summer months, and on fine days in Autumn, when the deeps are curled with a fine breeze, pike are to be taken very pleasantly by means of the artificial fly. The best imitation is a very large one of the Dragon Fly. I have seen nondescript large gaudy flies kill Pike well, and Mr Blacker, of Dean Street, Soho, is the best dresser of them I know. An imitation of the sand-martin or swallow dressed by means of feathers on a large hook, will prove an attractive bait for Pike in the seasons last mentioned.'

If I needed to be further convinced that this was an interesting 'method', I only had to look up the third edition of David Foster's *The Scientific Angler* and savour the following paragraph: 'The largest fish seem most partial to the fly; whether it is that they are hunger-bitten, or whether they rise in the spirit of wantonness, we cannot presume to say.'

Being quite partial to a 'wanton rise', my next decision was to choose a location with maximum potential. After a few phone calls, I was on a plane to Scotland. It's strange that the name of one of Scotland's greatest tourist attractions should be the butt of so many 'cheesy' old jokes. When asked where I had decided to fish, and replied "the Trossachs," I was greeted by a positive barrage of side-splitting 'one liners' including, "Don't worry, you can get an ointment for that," the inevitable "ooh nasty" and the all-time classic, "No need for that mate! . . . Where are you going fishing?"

If fishing is a 'plateau' sport, I'm still scrabbling up the side of the hill when it comes to the business of casting enormous pike flies, and as I drove the forty-five minute journey from Glasgow airport, I was not cherishing the thought of chucking half a rabbit into the teeth of a Scottish headwind. I needn't have worried. Greeted by head bailiff of the Trossachs Fisheries, Morris Meikle and guide Barrie Duffy, my mind was put at rest as Barrie explained he had developed light pike flies made of American materials. Unlike rabbit skin, they don't take on water.

I'm glad to say the same can be said of the excellent boats with their mandatory electric engines, which make for grief free outings. There's something about being propelled almost silently across a loch and having Rob Roy's house pointed out to you, that gives the day that extra dimension. We fished three lochs – Achray, Katrine and Venachar. I don't

think any of the fish we caught weighed more than ten pounds, but just being there and getting the casting right was reward enough. My Orvis 9-foot 9-weight rod and line were forgiving, and providing my 'double haul' didn't lose rhythm, all was well.

After the first couple of hours of 'chuck and duck' I got into my stride and managed to have a conversation with Barrie. He has caught pike up to thirty-one pounds on these 'fly only' lochs, and as the Scottish representative for the Pike Fly Fishing Association, is keen to encourage like-minded souls to sample the delights of the area.

On the last day of my trip, the weather turned, and I found myself casting into one of those torrential downpours that are referred to locally as 'highland mist!' I was about to suggest that we headed for the shore, when I got a ferocious take. The first run took most of the line off the reel, and I was already mentally posing with a 20-pounder. It was almost to the boat when it came off in a weed bed. Then I'm afraid, it happened. I fell into the trap! Instead of shrugging off the disaster, I threw my rod into the bottom of the boat and shouted out the title of this article!

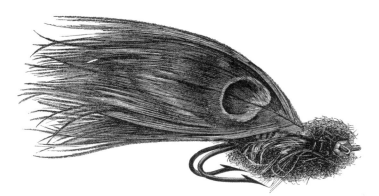

Right: Pike fly from Cholmondeley-Pennell's The Book of the Pike.

Below: Pike fly from The Journal of A. J. Lane.

Rest Assured

When my grandad took me fishing I was taught to always hold the rod, even when 'on the lead'. The only time I was advised to put it down was when we were fishing floating crust, because being a bit on the eager side, I would often strike too soon. Those precious few seconds between the fish taking and the rod being lifted from its improvised rest, were enough to ensure the bait had been truly taken.

I only kept a few of the V-shaped rests that Grandad cut with his penknife. These were usually of the stouter variety and were secretly turned into catapults and hidden behind the garden shed. Grandad's penknife was a wondrous 'machine' which I was only allowed to examine perhaps twice a year. Most of the thirty-two tools and blades that folded neatly into their horn-sided housing were used for cleaning and reaming his pipe; but one, a long curved implement, was always the cause of great intrigue and amusement. Every time I asked what it was used for, Grandad came up with a different answer. These ranged from 'getting stones out of horses' hooves', to 'hanging on to cliff faces'. Eventually, in a conspiratorial admission, he swore me to secrecy and explained that the strange metal probe was actually 'for getting broken cashew nuts out of alarm clocks!'

Another of the tools was a small saw and it was with this that he would occasionally cut us both a rod rest. Any of the metal rests available in our local tackle shop were considered 'a waste of hard-earned money.' Being the recipient of sixpence a week pocket money, I had to agree!

It's surprising to note, that between 1856 and 1951, no less than eighteen rod rests were patented in the UK. In 1895, Malloch of Perth, famous for the side-caster reel, patented a splendid three-rod rest which clamped to the back of the angler's boat for harling. The others, almost without exception, were designed for fishing from the bank.

Today, of course, we have folding stainless steel rod pods which hold up to four electronic bite-alarms with attendant swingers, springers and isotope bobbins. Being a self confessed 'tackle tart', I own quite a lot of this paraphernalia, but have,

of late, been trying to fish with a more minimalist approach. This has nothing to do with the fact that finding the energy to lug half a tackle shop up the bank doesn't get any easier! My determination to 'lighten up' has recently been rewarded with a 20lb 4oz common carp from the Hampshire Avon. *[Photograph withheld due to sheer jealousy by the publisher]* So perhaps it's time to take all that other 'stuff' down to the car boot sale.

Finally, while thumbing through some old copies of *Angling* magazine (circa 1941), I found this shot (above) of an unknown angler who definitely had the right idea. I'm told further developments

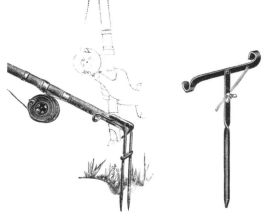

included the penile rod rest and the testicular bite-alarm! Thankfully, there is no photographic evidence available!

"Lose the handbrake, mate!"

I've just returned from possibly the best six weeks of my life! My wife Gelly and I travelled to Los Angeles, New Zealand, Australia, Tasmania and Singapore. One month of the trip was spent on a 'whistle-stop' tour of the North and South islands of New Zealand. Travel one day, fish the next, then move on.

Accommodation was in 'homestays' which I suppose are considered to be upmarket B&Bs. We soon got into the travelling routine, and having caught some phenomenal rainbow trout in the headwaters of Lake Taupo on the North Island, our second week found us gazing in disbelief at the breathtaking beauty of Lake Tekapo on the South Island. Its ice-blue waters were obviously going to be one of the highlights of the trip, providing we could get the fish to oblige.

Breakfast in a homestay is generally included in the price, but a word of warning. If like me, you are a PBP (Private Breakfast Person), beware the communal breakfast. On our first morning at Tekapo, we were greeted at the ten-seater table by three middle-aged Japanese ladies who obviously hadn't eaten for a fortnight, a Norwegian couple who conversed heatedly in their own language, an American gentleman who insisted on giving me a detailed account of his bass fishing in Florida and finally an English couple, both of whom were teachers.

I'd no sooner taken the top off my boiled egg when Mrs Teacher, leaning forward and fixing me with a half smile and an intense stare asked, "Tell me . . . do you think fish feel pain?" My wife, knowing that my standard reply to this question is always, 'What's the point of a hobby, unless someone gets hurt?' jumped in and saved the day, explaining that, "Fish don't have a nervous system like ours and tests have shown that they do not register pain as we do." She also gave the assembled company her discourse on the value of angling with regard to conservation of the waters. Mr Teacher asked for the marmalade and the Norwegians continued to argue in their mother tongue. When they paused for breath, I heard myself say, "Absolutely!" which seemed to deflate the argument.

The next memorable moment came when our hostess asked us all how we were going to spend the day. I was just about to say, "Well, I thought first off, I would remove the wife's appendix, then go and expose myself to a few Japanese tourist coaches," when a ring at the doorbell announced the arrival of our fishing guide Barry, who had just pulled up in his 4x4 truck. Professional guides in New Zealand are, quite frankly, among the best in the world, and they come 'fully loaded' with rods, reels, lunch, waders, bug repellent and sun screen.

Guiding on the islands is a highly competitive business, so a journey of at least an hour along rough wilderness tracks to secret locations is usually the order of the day. The track on this particular day finally petered out in a maze of rivulets, backwaters, pools and fast-moving streams. At one point, as we forded a particularly deep channel, I noticed the water was creeping under the doors! Barry, noting my concern said, "Don't worry mate, she floats like a boat." Eventually we parked on a high shingle ridge, got the cameras and rods together and hiked off deeper into the wilderness. Moving cautiously along side streams, Barry reminded us never to move ahead of him lest we disturb the fish. "There's not many of them," he said, "but they're big and wily."

Linking arms we waded waist-deep across fast-moving streams, clambered through gorse bushes and slid down steep shingle banks until Barry suddenly held up his hand like an Indian scout and pointed at a huge dark shape in slack water a few yards from the raging torrent of the main river.

"He's eating blow flies," said Barry, "you call them bluebottles . . . here . . ." He handed me a wonderful imitation with a bright blue body and hooped holographic wings.

I crept slowly into the water behind the fish. Barry whispered, "Remember, if the fly drags even three or four inches left or right, the fish won't look at it, only a perfect drift will give you a chance."

The first cast was rubbish, landing too far to the right and drifting away from the fish. The second was too short, with the fly dropping almost on top of it, but the third was perfect. The fly landed six feet in front of the fish, which rose and sipped down the bluebottle; I muttered, "God save the Queen,"

raised the rod and it was on. But only for a moment. Before I could say 'gotcha' it shot into the main river, wrapped the line around a root wad and was gone! I looked at Barry, he looked at me and shrugged.

"What happened?" I said. Barry thought for a moment and replied, "Well, when they move that fast, it gets a bit technical," which I later realised is guide speak for 'you were too bleedin' slow mate!'

The rest of the morning was one of the sharpest learning curves I've ever experienced. Having to mend the line quickly when the water is moving in two, sometimes three directions, can be immensely frustrating. As the water crashes around rocks causing 'speed lanes' and back eddies, controlling the line requires a degree of concentration which I don't always find easy. When I did get the drift right, I was often too late striking the nymph or too quick on the dry. I managed two small browns and a rainbow by mid-morning and handed the rod to Gelly, who of course proceeded to catch two larger fish by the time we stopped for lunch!

The afternoon started quietly, but just as we thought about heading back to our homestay, we came upon what looked like a three-acre stillwater. The river in full flood had scoured out a huge pool. When the water subsided, it had left entrance and exit channels so that fish not willing to fight the current of the main river could rest and feed at their leisure. The problem was that we spooked at least three fish before we could get within casting range.

Eventually a huge sipping 'submarine' started to move towards us. I cast, he inspected the offering and moved away at speed. We crept along the bank and crouched down waiting for the fish to return. After twenty minutes or so, he came back.

"He's eating tiny spinners," said Barry, handing me a size 16 example that I could hardly see! "Cast to him sitting down, put the fly six feet to his left," came the hushed instruction. "But there's a fence behind me," I whispered. "Get on with it mate," said Barry.

More by luck than judgement, I managed the cast. The fish saw the fly land and shot across and ate it without inspection. "God save the Queen!" I shouted and we all stood up! The fly held, the 5lb tippet held, and I held my breath when Barry eventually netted a beautiful 10lb 4oz brown trout. Gelly caught the whole thing on video and shot

the stills. Barry was ecstatic! He hadn't had a client catch a double for about six weeks. And me? I looked around and thought, well, it wasn't a bad cast . . . It was a magnificent fish, but what made it extra special was to have had the good fortune to catch it in these stunning surroundings.

As we made our way back to the 4x4 Barry said, "It was good to take out a husband and wife who both fish. Quite often," he explained, "the wife or girlfriend gets bored and starts asking where she can get a cappuccino or a proper toilet."

"What do you do in those circumstances?" I asked. "Well . . . if it gets really bad, I take the client on one side and say, 'Any chance we could lose the handbrake, mate?' "

Thank you New Zealand, it was wonderful!

47

The Totally Tasteless Teapot Award

Now that Christmas is over, let me ask you . . . 'How was your smile?' You know the one I mean . . . it's the one you bring out every Christmas when you have to open that present! Sure enough, Auntie Wyn and Uncle Reg smile back and say in unison, "It's from both of us." But you knew that it was from them. You recognise the wrapping paper! Auntie hasn't bought any new paper since she slipped and hurt her head the day sweets came off the ration!

Your fingers tremble, your mind races. What was it last year? . . . Oh yes, fisherman's underpants with 'Catch you later' across the bum. Absolutely sodding hilarious! Nothing for it now, better open up. Undo the ribbon, no sellotape here, might spoil the paper. And there it is . . . The Fisherman's Alarm Clock! . . . A polystyrene creel with a clock forced into its front, the hands of which are two unrecognisable fish, and the sweeping second-hand is - yes, you've guessed it - a fishing rod! These three indicators of time emanate from the angler's stomach pictured on the face, as he gazes out over a river which is obviously somewhere on Venus!

What's going on? Surely, whatever your hobby, people only have to ask? "Hello Eric, I know you like chicken sexing, would you like the gauntlets, the magnifying goggles or the anti-fowl pest wipe?"

There is now a thriving industry producing angling-associated gifts which are bought by people who don't angle, but know someone who does. Some of these knick-knacks are OK; I have no objection to the fishing mug. I'm quite attached to the odd fish-themed tea towel. I even have a lurid trout tie which I wear when any invitation insists on 'jacket and tie'. But a fish-shaped pen? A fisherman's egg cup? A large-mouth bass in the shape of a baseball cap?

Where will it end? Fisherman's condoms?! "Will that be the perch or the Moray eel model, Sir?"

What's wrong with books? I make a conscious effort not to buy any new angling books after 1st September. Discreet enquiries were made this year and, joy of joys, Santa made sure that Jon Beer's new book *Gone Fishing* (a collection of his recent articles), was in my Christmas stocking. My other present was the flu. Jon's hilarious book should carry a health warning; I laughed so much, it was confiscated twice for fear of a fatal coughing fit!

I suppose my secret problem with tasteless angling gifts is, that they're not quite tasteless enough. I mean, come on chaps, where's the angler's posing pouch with the 'Dayglo' leaping salmon? Where's the talking loo-roll that tells risqué fishing stories? Or the Whoopee cushion in the shape of a record carp? Where can I acquire those gifts so truly awful that, suddenly they're not? I need to know and, to help you over any embarrassment, I have devised an irresistible competition . . . I want readers to give kitsch a capital 'K'. Find your most tasteless gift and photograph it in all its gaudy glory! Model it, if you're that way inclined, but remember, it must be really bad. Send

your details and photograph to the publisher of this fine tome.

The publisher's decision is dependent, as always, on how much alcoholic refreshment he's offered. Oh yes . . . the prize? There isn't one, but if this book ever makes a second edition, he promises to include the worst entries. To stand a chance, your entry will have to be in much worse taste than these delightful salutes to angling in the twenty-first century.

The publisher sent me the teapot below as an example of something that is not only totally tasteless but totally useless. Surely the one thing an ugly teapot can do is make tea. Not so. Upon opening the lid of the creel we found the following note:

VERY IMPORTANT

THIS IS AN ORNAMENTAL PRODUCT
FOR DECORATIVE PURPOSES ONLY
IT MUST NOT BE USED AS A TEAPOT

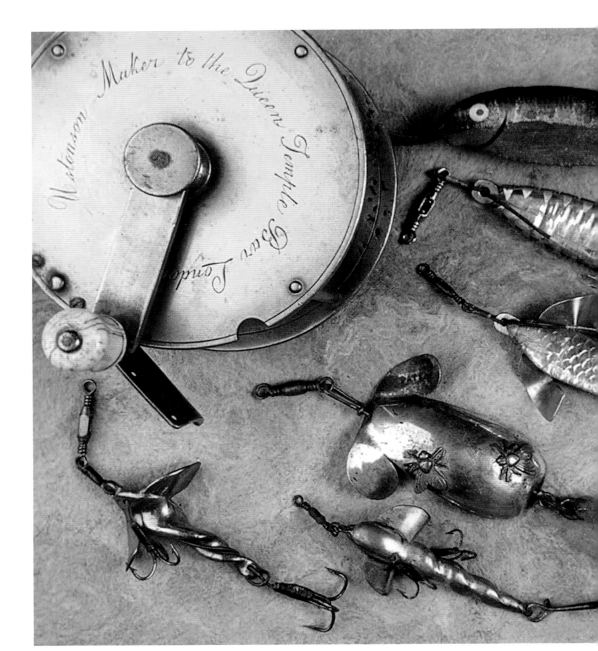

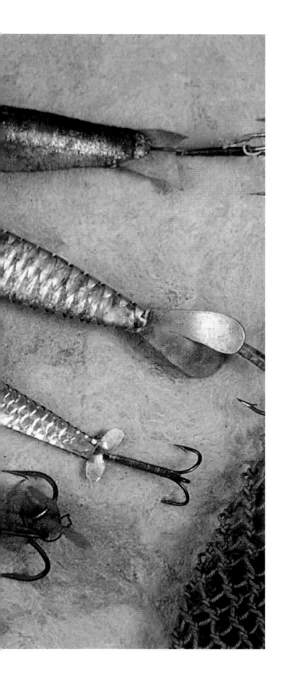

Lure of the Lure

I forget exactly when it was that I acquired my first lure. I've been collecting vintage tackle for about twelve years and when I began, I put one or two aside, promising myself that eventually I would try to discover something of their origins. My initial interest was in early fixed-spool reels and cane coarse rods. Then Aerial and Nottingham centre-pins tempted me for a few years and this led, not surprisingly, to early brass reels and all manner of ephemera.

I suppose the bug truly bit when I attended an auction in Devon in 1991. I had driven down to try to purchase a couple of very early Coxon Aerial reels when I discovered, under one of the trestle tables in the viewing room, three boxes full of what was described as 'various angling items including floats, artificial baits, hooks, line and traces'. In those days there were only three serious collectors of lures, and one of them was keeping a watchful eye on me as I rifled through these early treasures. I lost count of the baits after about a hundred, and the floats were so early, and in such perfect condition, I knew I must try to buy them.

The auction began and I managed to buy one of the Aerials. When the three boxes came up, I thought I'd be able to buy them for about £80, but the lure collector at the back of the room took the bidding to £290 without pausing. I remember thinking, 'Right, so now I'm a lure collector!' The room went very quiet and I eventually made a final bid of £360. There was a great deal of muttering from the assembled company including the inevitable, 'He must be mad', but the contents of those boxes are still one of the best buys I have ever made. There was a total of forty floats, a hundred and sixty-two lures and enough old traces to refurnish any that required attention. It soon became clear that the previous owner of this historic hoard must have been squirrelling stuff away from around the turn of the century to about 1930.

Now I was hooked! Whenever I saw a lure I hadn't seen before, I tried to buy it. I drove hundreds of miles in search of early examples and pestered the catalogue and book collectors for photocopies of any relevant information on the subject. Five years, and an equal number of bulging box-files later, I sat down one rainy Sunday to try to collate this material into some semblance of order. The

first thing that struck me was that, for any given year, retailers' catalogues mostly carried the same selection of lures (obviously supplied by the same manufacturing wholesaler). The most famous of these was James Gregory, whose biggest customer was Allcock & Co. Up to the turn of the last century, many of their metal baits were supplied by Gregory from his workshops in the jewellery manufacturing district of Birmingham. Most of these early examples have glass eyes and beautiful body engraving which owes more to the jeweller's art than to the angler's invention.

Old copies of the *Fishing Gazette* gave me an accurate fix on Gregory's work, but examination of early patent specifications revealed that many of his baits retailed by Allcock & Co, and marked 'patent', were never supported by an application. Despite this confusion, I decided that the only way to assemble an accurate and informative chronology was to base it on the registration of patents, from the first in 1867 through to the 1930s. More than one hundred residents of the British Isles patented lures during this period, the most prolific being Philip Geen of Richmond in Surrey. He registered no less than nine innovations between 1889 and 1910. He was

President of the London Anglers' Association for over twenty years and was the author of *What I Have Seen While Fishing & How I Have Caught My Fish.* Constant review of his work in the *Fishing Gazette* guaranteed him a high profile and most of the major tackle firms, including Farlows and Hardy Brothers, stocked at least one of his baits. The ingenuity, popularity and quality of his lures ensured that many have survived, and mint examples can sometimes be found still sewn to their tradecards and in their original boxes.

I am quite sure that if some of these patterns were reproduced today they would once again enjoy enormous popularity. I have tried most of Mr Geen's lures in the pool of a fast-flowing brook near my home and their action is more than convincing. It does well to remember that these baits caught thousands of fish in the early 1900s without the aid of 'Dayglo' tassles or manufactured colours never seen below the waterline.

Compiling my book *The Best of British Baits* has been an enjoyable task although I have had to be wary of that most dangerous of collector afflictions: 'anoracksia'. Tackle bores are to be avoided at all costs and, luckily, there are a few patent

specifications that guarantee that one takes neither the subject nor oneself too seriously. Two of my favourites are: firstly, the 'Gas-bladder Minnow' invented by Mrs Margaret White from Glasgow in 1920 – her patent specification gives all manner of detail but no clue as to how she actually inflated it! (suggestions on a postcard to the publisher please!); secondly, 'The Natural Smell Bait' – an aluminium Devon with a perforated hollow body, into which it was recommended that you stuff 'squashed minnow, prawn, aniseed etc' (just the sort of thing to have in your pocket when you visit the pub after a long, hot day on the river.)

We are not traditionally a nation of lure anglers, and the practice of spinning is, in fact, frowned upon by a great number of game-fishing purists. I hope, however, that readers will share my enthusiasm for the humble lure and appreciate the ingenuity and craftsmanship that can be found in this area of our angling heritage.

Twitching Prawns

6

I was more than surprised . . . I cast a large prawn to within two feet of the nose of the 80lb lemon shark, gave it a couple of slow pulses, then watched in amazement as the shark accepted my breakfast offering, felt the hook and roared off towards the horizon. Fifteen minutes later I had it alongside the boat for a swift unhooking and a fond farewell.

The barracuda was apprehended in the same manner except that the movement of the prawn was more staccato. It's all part of the extraordinary behaviour of prawns (or shrimp as they are known) in the back country of the Florida Keys. Our guide, Captain Jim Perry, was most insistent that each species is attracted by a different movement. I asked him, "When not attached to a hook, how does the shrimp know how to behave when it's feeling suicidal?" Captain Jim narrowed his eyes, gazed towards the horizon and muttered ". . . At advanced guide school, they said we didn't have to answer that question!"

It was the eighth year my wife Gelly and I had fished amongst the three hundred square miles of mangroved back country, that stretches from Marathon in the centre of the Keys down to Key West. Two and a half hours south from Miami finds us at Parmers Resort a small motel on Little Torch Key, twenty-five miles north of Key West. Our routine rarely varies: a speedy unpack, a quick shower and five minutes back up Highway One to K.D.'s Steak and Sea Food Restaurant on Big Pine Key. A bottle of Chardonnay, a house salad with blue cheese dressing followed by blackened snapper (with real Cajun spices) and a double baked potato.

The waitress tells us to have 'a beautiful evening,' so now all is right with the world except for . . . the local weather forecast. A low front is moving in and for the next four days the wind blows twenty knots and it rains at least once a day. We shop 'til we drop, (my prize purchase was a fantastic 12-inch garfish fly!) and commiserate with the other anglers.

On the fourth day we brave the elements from 7am until 1pm and have some wonderful fishing. Although the wind is still high, making the fly rod redundant, Captain Jim guides us to some secret 'hidy holes' where we find the shark and barracuda. We fish every morning for four days casting shrimp and surface plugs, contending with a wind that rarely gives us any peace, but as they say in all the best stories '. . . we returned home tired but happy'.

On the last day the wind dropped a little and I decided to take out the fly rod. I always thought my fly casting was pretty cool until I tried it on a flats boat. Watching anglers who have mastered the necessary technique is a humbling experience. They seem to effortlessly 'double haul' more line than I've got on any of my reels into the teeth of a medium sized hurricane.

You hope and pray that the wind stays away and you can pull off at least one accurate cast. I stood on the bow looking nonchalant, sweat dripping down my polaroids as I tried to see the fish before Jim spotted them. But he was poling us across the flats standing on a four-foot platform on the back of the boat with a bird's eye view.

The moment I thought a beer might be in order Jim said, "Chris . . . two bonefish . . . 2 o'clock . . . thirty yards . . . cast!" Suddenly I can't tell the time . . . and what's the difference between twenty and thirty yards? I cast far too quickly, forgetting I was using a heavy fly which, instead of sailing in perfect flight over my head, came back level with it and lodged itself securely in the back of my $5 straw hat! The two bonefish are now in Mexico. Have you ever heard a bonefish laugh?

Fly casting in salt water is a bit like skiing. The moment you start to get it right it's time to come home.

Me, Captain Jim Perry and Barry the Cuda.

They Can't Touch You for it . . .

If you're into fondling your ancestor's old tackle, may I unreservedly recommend the Nottingham Clamp Winch. This 'clamper', to use a collector's term, is definitely in my 'tactile top ten'. There is something about the combination of brass and wood that can rival the cashmere cardigan or the silk edge on my security blanket.

The ivory handles and pillared drum core generate a certain 'frisson' whilst the brass clamp itself, with its screw-down tightening device, has to be experienced to be believed!

BARKER'S DELIGHT:

OR,

THE ART OF

ANGLING.

Wherein are discovered many rare secrets very necessary to be known by all that delight in that Recreation, both for catching the Fish, and dressing thereof.

The Second EDITION much enlarged.

By *THOMAS BARKER*, an ancient practitioner in the said Art.

ECCLES. 3. I. II.

There is a time and season to every purpose under heaven: Every thing is beautiful in his time.

LONDON:

Printed by *J. G.* for *Richard Marriot*, and are to be sold at his shop in S. *Dunstans* Church-yard Fleetstreet. 1657.

The first clue to the existence of a 'spring' or 'clamp' on a reel or 'wind', comes in the second edition of Charles Barker's book *Barker's Delight* (1657). When advising us on salmon fishing he comments, 'You must have your Winder within two foot of the bottom to go on your rod made in this manner, with a spring, that you may put it on as low as you please'.

The next reference that I can find is two hundred years later in William Bailey's *The Anglers Instructor* (1857) where he tells us that for barbel fishing, one's reel '. . . should be a three and a half inch common wood one, varnished to keep the rain from swelling the wood, without too much brass about it, except the slide or hoop for fastening the rod'.

J. T. Burgess in the first edition of his book *Angling* (1867) recommends this type of reel but warns it can sometimes run '. . . too free'. Nonetheless he tells us that they could be found for sale at the emporium of a '. . . Mr Rider of 48 Ellis Street, Birmingham'.

Wherever you find your Nottingham Clamp Winch, don't be afraid to fondle . . . they can't touch you for it!

Mallochs . . . !

Next time you nonchalantly flick open the bale-arm of your fixed-spool reel and cast with unerring accuracy to a fish that has just 'dimpled' close to the far bank, spare a thought for our angling ancestors.

Before the mid 1800s casting from the reel fell neatly into two categories. 'Blinding Skill' or 'Bugger's Muddle'. It was on 28th May, 1878, that a Mr G. R. Holding registered a patent for a reel with a swivelling foot. This allowed the angler to turn the reel to the forward facing position for casting, and back to the original position, for winding in or playing his catch. Before this time most anglers were obliged to pull line from their brass or wooden reel, offer a prayer that the wind would not blow it into nearby vegetation, and swing the bait out over the water.

Although a few simple wooden reels have been found bearing Holding's name, it's safe to say that his invention was not a commercial success. It was not until tackle manufacturer, P. D. Malloch of Perth patented his sidecaster on 3rd September, 1884, that anglers embraced this new casting concept. What possessed Malloch to call his reel a 'sidecaster' rather than a 'frontcaster' we'll never know. Perhaps he was preoccupied with the problem of line twist which plagued these early solid brass reels and was the subject of many complaints and bad press. He cured this unfortunate fault by providing the reel with a removable spool, which the angler could reverse every half dozen or so casts, thus eliminating any twist in the line.

Sales then went from strength to strength but, not satisfied with the reel's success, the company continued to make improvements. Early examples had no locking mechanism to hold the spool in position when casting. Later models had a small sliding stud but by 1927, most were fitted with a 'Gibbs' lever which proved to be the most popular solution.

The rarest Malloch sidecasters are the multiplying variety. The first example appeared in 1912 and was hailed as 'a time saver for the bait angler'. The second model the 'Multi Malloch' was catalogued around 1925 and claimed to have

' . . . solved all the problems associated with multiplying reels,' and 'opened up a new field of interest for the spinning enthusiast'.

I'm very grateful to Mr Malloch and those innovative thinkers who followed in his footsteps inventing and refining the fixed–spool reels we use today. Centre–pins and modern multipliers are all very well but my Mitchell 300 always seems to know what it's doing!

Mousing for Leopards

Lower base camp on the Kanektok river in Alaska is about seven thousand miles from my front door. It's so far west it's almost east! The first leg was Gatwick to New York and then on to Anchorage. Here we spent the night and felt it our duty to visit the 'Great Alaskan Bush Company'. Ironically, none of the young ladies who 'dance' there had a 'bush' of any kind. Perhaps they're confiscated during rehearsals?!

Our flight the next morning took us to Bethel which is the last outpost of civilisation before the final 'hop' to Quinhagak. Here, luggage and passengers are loaded into half a dozen flat-bottomed fishing skiffs in preparation for our journey upriver. Before leaving, one of our group asked 'Buzz', who runs the local store, if the mosquitoes on the river were big. Having been asked the same question hundreds of times 'Buzz' pretended to think for a moment and once he had everyone's attention said, "Big? . . . I'll tell ya . . . if one was standing flat footed it could ★★★★ a turkey!"

The fifteen-mile journey upriver to our camp took about thirty minutes and was not for the faint-hearted. Our guide and boatman who rejoiced in the name of 'Rhino' ("Why do they call you Rhino?" - "'Cos that's my name Sir!"),

gunned the outboard to full power and every time we came to a shallow run would push down a huge metal bar attached to a hinged device which lifted the engine almost out of the water.

The camp accommodates twelve anglers, seven guides and a cook. There are twelve two-man tents, one mess tent, one shower tent and two toilets. As we stepped ashore I thought my glasses needed cleaning but soon realised the air was filled with mosquitoes. Five minutes later a strong breeze sprang up and they were gone. They were big but no threat to a turkey!

Before moving on to the wonderful six days' fishing we had on the Kanektok, a word about the camp toilets. If you are in the habit of spending rather too long on the porcelain throne, these tented chambers will cure you in minutes. First you must spray them with insecticide, zip the door shut and wait for the sound of falling bodies. Once you've rushed in and re-zipped the door the last thing you want to do is get comfortable. Why? Because they don't flush! Every two days the toilet seat is exchanged for a metal cover which is clamped shut. The chimney that protrudes from the back of the toilet tent gives you your first clue that you are having an intimate relationship

with a propane fired oven. All waste is burnt off to guarantee that there is no contamination of the environment or the water. Once you get in to the routine, your timing improves and you do your best to arrive after 'burn off'. Mind you, get there too early and you're definitely in the 'hot seat'.

The tented accommodation is good. I shared with casting instructor and trip organiser, Peter Cockwill, which was fine until I discovered he snores for England!

Each day begins with a huge breakfast during which you are allocated a guide. Each pair of anglers fishes with a different guide each day which gives everyone a broad understanding of the river and its many species. The main targets are king salmon, chum, sockeye and char. These were all exciting to catch but of greater interest to me were the leopard rainbow trout and the Arctic grayling. The Kanektok is a fly-only river where barbless hooks, and catch and release is the order of the day. A 9–weight outfit fishing 'teeny' nymphs on a mini sink–tip line seems to get the best results when targeting the salmon. The 'leopards' were another story. 'Mousing' for these spectacular fish is an experience I can't wait to repeat. Using a deer hair imitation of our little furry friends you cast your 'fly' (make no mistake you are 'matching the hatch!') on to the opposite bank, 'jig' it into the water and as it hurtles downstream there's more than a good chance that one of the most exquisite trout you have ever seen will give you a heart stopping take.

Challenging these trout in the local beauty contest are the Arctic grayling which have been caught to over three pounds.

My most physically challenging moment of the trip was on the first day when we were fishing for 'kings'. I hadn't been doing too well until Peter Cockwill came to the rescue with a few timely tips. He was still explaining the best technique when something which felt like a jet-propelled sofa took my fly and headed upstream. We were fishing on a long gravel bar which allows you to play the fish for quite a time as you move up trying to bring it in to the shallows. When you reach the end of the gravel there is no alternative but to jump in the boat and chase the fish up to the next bar. This happened three times and took forty minutes before our guide was able to tail my first king salmon in the shallows. It weighed 37lb and was a 'chrome' bright fish that hadn't been out of the sea for more than a day. When we returned it I just sat in the water not really believing what had just happened.

Our guide on that remarkable day was Brad Duncan, son of Dave Duncan who pioneered angling on the Kanektok back in the early Seventies. Brad and his team now run this business that specialises in remote wilderness fishing. Their care of the environment, the local community and their guests is a model from which we could all learn. As I started my journey back to the UK I thought how apt that American 'one-liner' is that goes, 'missing you already'.

Les Carpistes Entrepide!

I didn't really want to write a 'no fish' article, but that was the way it was beginning to look as we set off for our annual holiday in France. The copy date loomed ever nearer and none of my recent adventures had produced a decent fish, let alone a jolly anecdote.

A day on Loch Derg, during the Angling Writer's Conference in Ireland, was a spectacular blank. Although, that evening I was the proud recipient of the runner-up prize for 'Humorous Writer of the Year'. This award turned out to be a 'yawning' pike's head mounted on a board. Nice but not thrilling!

I returned to Ireland two weeks later and battled with five-foot waves on Loch Corrib which rewarded me with two small pike. Scotland was worse. Five of us spent three days on the Tummel without annoying a single salmon. The river Avon was not much better. A few small browns no more than half a pound each; the only highlight being a 12lb carp on my fly rod using a deer hair 'muddler' with a strong resemblance to a trout pellet!

Then in early June, my wife and I packed the car with enough tackle to stock a small shop, plus all the holiday essentials needed for a fortnight in a wonderful French gite with its own eight-acre lake. I remember thinking on our journey south, that if I didn't catch anything during our holiday, *Waterlog* readers would be receiving my thesis on the Mitchell 300 bale-arm spring (Mark II!).

The overnight ferry to St Malo is efficient and the drive to our destination between Bordeaux and Toulouse is tiring, but who cares! The lakes were waiting and the phone calls before we left assured us the carp were feeding. Up to a few years ago the farmer who owns the property was apt to catch the odd carp and slip it onto the barbecue, but now that he's made the mystifying discovery that Englishmen pay good money to catch the carp and put them back, everything has changed.

The weather during our first week was not the best. Overcast, humid and one night, we were treated to three inches of rain. But our catch rate was quite good. Five tench, three bream, three carp, two trees and an underwater snag that appeared to be the size of Marble Arch. The heaviest carp was a 33lb mirror, but the prettiest was a 19lb common. All caught on maize.

Every time I fish our French lake I bring at least ten pounds of 'Super Pongo – Low Fat, High Priced, Nose Curling, Flavour Leeching, Life Enhancing, Deadly Secret Boilies' only to find the carp like maize! Mixed with a stiff groundbait rolled into small balls, left to dry in the sun and then catapulted towards the hook baits, it seems to do the trick.

However, there was a problem. There are about a hundred and fifty carp in this lake but I had convinced myself that most of them lived under the lily pads just beyond the range of my catapult elastic.

Using both my French words I explained my problem to the farmer. "*Nous avons un aqua tricycle pour les Carpistes Entrepides!*" he said and pointed down the lake. Of course . . . I'd forgotten!

Tethered to the bank behind a large bush, I found the wondrous machine. Three vast blue plastic buoyant wheels which act as floats. Two saddles, one for the passenger and one for the peddler. Attached to each of the rear wheel/floats are small paddles which, as you peddle, propel you across the water.

I had rediscovered this fine angling accessory just in time for a visit from my good friend, broadcaster Mike Allan. For the last three years we'd been concentrating on our fly fishing, but as soon as he saw this mini French Redmire, all the old enthusiasms returned.

Maize was peddled to every likely looking spot and casts were made with increasing accuracy and fervour. Then the weather cheered up, temperatures reached 90 degrees and the carp went to sleep. Mike managed a 20-pounder early one evening but apart from that, it was deadly. Obviously night fishing was the answer but frankly the local restaurants are too good to miss and our French dinners, with far too much regional wine,

are just as important as the fishing. A good night's sleep also ranks high on my 'most wanted' list.

On our last day my wife came to the rescue and offered to cook dinner so we could eat within grabbing distance of the rods.

My first run at 9.30 broke the line in the 'Marble Arch' snag. My second at 10.30, came off after three or four minutes and it was not until 11.45 that a wonderful 31lb common decided that maize was on the menu.

On the drive home it suddenly struck me that perhaps the sound of the mighty water tricycle could have put the fish down during the day. But what the hell! It caused much merriment and to me, the laughter of friends and family is much more important than what you catch.

Gagging for it!

Pike Scissors

Earlier this year, a large pike got my favourite plug stuck half way down its neck, and try as I might I couldn't get its mouth open. I even turned it on its back to see if disorientation would do the trick, but it had obviously decided to meet its maker with sealed lips! I finally tried to open its jaws by hand, wearing a green re-inforced rubber

Allcock Gag

gardening glove. The trap eased a fraction then snapped shut again. I whipped my hand out of range but left the glove clamped between its front teeth. So now it had my plug and my glove. There was only one thing for it . . . retrieve the glove. As I pulled tentatively on the wrist-band - a miracle! The jaws slowly opened, the barbless trebles were easily removed and all was well. Returning the fish was another drama mostly to do with treading on my sandwiches!

When my adrenalin levels finally

returned to normal, it struck me, that it is hardly surprising that our fore-fathers invented such an array of jaw-prising, hook-removing and cranium-coshing apparatus. The most eminently sensible of these are without doubt pike scissors.

They appear in retail catalogues from the early 1880s. In *The Modern Angler* by Otter (1898) their praises were sung as follows: *'I have found the pike gag of great assistance when disengaging the hooks. It shuts up like a pair of scissors and when in use, the points are inserted in the mouth of the pike, which can be opened to the required extent by means of the bows fitting on the finger and thumb. The gag is kept open by way of the steel extender, the teeth of which are made to catch on a screw; but when not in use, this portion shuts up on one limb of the gag. The pike gag can also be used as scissors, being very strong, and sharpened for the purpose.'*

A gadget that worked very much along the same lines was patented by Allcock & Co in December 1902. The specification read: *'Gag for holding the mouths of fish open while the hooks are extracted. It has ends which are inserted in the mouth. The gag being locked in to position by the perforated cross plate. Each arm is in two pieces hinged at the centre for folding up.'*

The 'Conway' combined pike 'Stunner' and disgorger also appeared in early Allcock catalogues under 'sundries'. As this was basically a fork-ended cosh they gave few details, except that it was $12^1/4$ inches long, had a screw lead button, a bronzed socket and a beaded-wood grip that was stained and polished. The price was a very reasonable 2/9d.

Slightly more expensive at 8/6d, plus 3d postage, you could send off to Farlows for the magnificent Jardine gag patented in 1896. Farlows' 1909 catalogue tells us that *'. . . by turning the handle, the mouth of the fish can be distended to any width required'*.

Perhaps I should have taken my Jardine gag with me on my piking trip. On second thoughts, two sets of trebles are enough pointed objects in any fish's mouth.

THE "JARDINE" GAG (Patent).

I'll Never Do it!

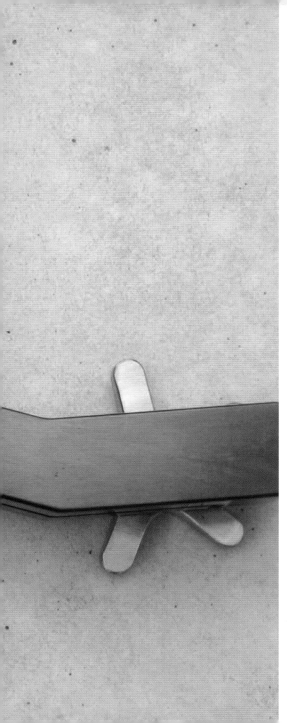

Lots of people do it, but frankly, I'd never fancied it. In fact I'd stated quite categorically, that I'd never do it. "Why waste all that time when you could be fishing?" I'd said, "Tie my own flies - you must be joking!"

Then, in the autumn of 2003, I asked a life-changing question. I was standing in Peter Cockwill's fine fishing emporium in Albury, Surrey, and for some reason I was up at the 'quiet' end of the shop, where serious gentlemen were examining all manner of flotsam, fur and feather. At the other end, anglers spoke loudly of the virtues of this or that fly, emphasising their beliefs with exaggerated gestures indicating the length of captured fish and miming the moment the rod 'hooped' over.

At the quiet end, however, there was an oasis of calm. Words were rarely spoken, just an occasional grunt of satisfaction. If they did speak actual words, it was in an unfamiliar language : 'Bustard hackles', 'Head Cement', 'Half-hitch tool', 'Peacock sword', 'Hare's mask'.

I wanted to know more. Finally, the shop cleared, and Peter looked across at me in those unfamiliar surroundings and said, "You all right?" "Fine," I said, and then, indicating a wall of fly-tying products, "Could you teach me to do all this?"

There was a very long pause and finally Peter said, "Probably." That one word sealed my fate.

Six lessons later, I started to claw my way up the slippery slope towards the totally unattainable 'perfect' fly.

'Road kills' held a whole new fascination for me. I swapped a valuable antique reel for eight biscuit tins full of rare feathers and tying materials. I pestered the British fly-tying 'cognoscenti': Terry Griffiths, Steve Thornton and Alan Bithell all gave generously of their time and knowledge. When Alan noticed that I had enough tools and gadgets to stock a small shop he said, "Ah yes, I'm afraid it happens to us all. There's no cure . . . it's called 'gizmalogical gadgetitis'!"

I now have nearly forty fly-tying books and an unliftable pile of UK and American magazines which tell me how to tie everything from a classic 'Mayfly' to a rubber 'Squid'.

So now I'm a happy tyer, but my acquisitive nature will not let things rest. I search the vintage tackle auctions for rare feathers, old tying tools, silks and dubbings and was thrilled recently to find a fine example of a tying vice that was 'state of the art' in the late 1800s.

It was designed by Jacob Holtzapffel (1768-1885) who set up business in London as an ornamental lathe maker. The quality of his work was such that he only produced twenty lathes a year and his beautiful vices were a spin-off from the company's main production. Queen Victoria is said to have owned both a lathe and a vice.

You may be surprised to learn that the most treasured item on my tying table is not an antique. It is the L. A.W. vice designed by engineer, Lawrence A. Waldron, it is simply the 'best'. As one professional tyer told me, "The design is so perfect that you can't help but become a better tyer." At £400 I should hope so!

I have not, as yet, gone to the extreme of taking my tying outfit to the riverbank to try and exactly 'match the hatch'. If I did, I'm sure I'd favour the pocket-cosy 'Corkscrew Vice'. My model didn't come with any instructions but my suggestion to the manufacturers is as follows. *'Open bottle. Remove cork. Screw vice into nearby log. Drink contents of bottle. Tie fly. Sleep soundly'*

So, now as a fully-fledged member of

the 'vice squad' I look forward to an enjoyable future creating all manner of flying insects. Tyers with many year's experience tell me that the next exciting summit to be conquered is to tie a fully dressed salmon fly. But, as I rarely fish for salmon, all I can say is "I'll probably never do it . . . "

The Weird Weir

I fish with my friend Jeff about four or five times a year. Whether it's 'trouting' on the fly, or coarse fishing our local rivers, it's an experience I always enjoy. As one of the finest rod restorers I know, Jeff has little time for carbon or fibreglass and fishes almost exclusively with classic cane. So when he invited me to fish the 'Weird Weir' on the river Avon below Salisbury, I was intrigued to see which of his vast collection of cane rods he would produce to tame some of the huge pike we'd seen earlier in the year.

"There you are," he said, "have a go with that!" and handed me an immaculate J. B. Walker pike rod rigged with a *Fishing Gazette* bung and a deadbait.

The bung 'trotted' across the weir at a good rate and on only the second pass, held in the current momentarily, then dived under the surface.

"Let it run," called Jeff from the hut.

"No choice," I shouted back as the clutch on the reel screamed and the rod took on a life of its own.

Eventually the fish paused, I waited a moment, wound down and struck. The rig-less monofilament line flew through the air and landed in an untidy pile in the reeds. There was a very long silence. I looked at Jeff . . . he looked at me . . . we both looked at the end of the broken line. Jeff then made the only suggestion that one can make under such circumstances. "Cuppa tea?" he said.

I declined his offer and decided to set up a carp rod some twenty yards away. My ancient 'Delkim' bite-alarm would announce any enquiries from the big carp that sometimes visit the weir, while we could carry on trying for the pike.

I fixed a 'boilie', smelling of something I don't really want to talk about, to a simple hair-rig and hurled it out to where the circling pool met the white water. I added a few free offerings and returned to Jeff, muttering to myself that nothing was going to break 20lb braided line.

Not twenty minutes had passed, when the buzzer started slowly 'beeping', gaining momentum as I raced towards it. I struck - and stood there in utter disbelief as the braided line tumbled into a heap at my feet.

The severing of two different lines within an hour one can put down to coincidence, but when it happened a third time an hour later, I started to look around for the 'Candid Camera' hidden in the shrubbery! I wouldn't have been at all surprised if a frogman had emerged from the weir grinning and waving a pair of scissors!

"Cuppa tea?" Said Jeff.

"Definitely!" I said.

The day wore on, we lunched and in the afternoon I joined Jeff on the other side of the weir where he caught a beautiful 10lb barbel on one of his many Mk IV carp rods.

It was later in the day when we'd returned to the hut and Jeff was once again 'trotting' for the pike, when his chum Tony arrived. Tony Timms is something of a local hero because he holds the record for catching no less than thirty-six barbel out of the weir in just one day!

I was explaining to him the mystery of the severed line when Jeff suddenly said, "Hello what's this?"

"I think you've picked up someone else's line," said Tony and reaching forward untangled it from Jeff's rod tip. As he passed it back to me for inspection I said, "This is my line!" Tony turned to me and said, ". . . and it's your fish, too!"

Something rather large was about to try and pull us both into the river and might have succeeded, had it not been for Jeff's quick thinking. Cutting off his pike tackle he said, "Quick, give me the end of the line."

Now I don't know if you have ever tried to join braided to monofilament line but it is not a job for the faint-hearted, especially when your hands are wet and two anglers are hoping the fish won't charge off and remove their fingers! Jeff calmly made everything secure and wound the line on to the spool of his reel. Handing me the rod he said, "There you are then . . . your fish!"

It was only a few seconds later that the fish decided to 'wake up' and the knotted line started to clatter back and forth through the rod rings.

Eventually Tony ran forward with the net and said, "Hello, it's a big 'un!" It was in fact, an 18lb common carp. But who caught it? I'd say we all did!

As to the severed lines, they still remain a mystery. We all have our theories but as far as I'm concerned I'd like the frogman with the scissors to go and play somewhere else!

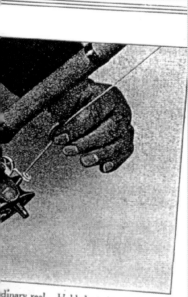

dinary reel. Hold the rod in the RIGHT
f first finger on outer edge of reel drum.
ine to the right, under end of eye, and
, don't "arrange" it.

trations showing
"BROWNIE"

When I first started collecting I was asked if I wanted a Milward's Brownie. I thought I was being offered some sort of exotic hash cake. No such luck! In 1921 Milwards launched, on an unsuspecting public, a reel whose instructions for use were so complex that I'm surprised it turned out to be as popular as it did. Today examples show up regularly in auction and any collector interested in oddities has one in his own collection.

The instruction book for this curious reel used eight photographs and 353 words to explain its complexities.

Milwards had a novel approach to the launch of the reel in the *Fishing Gazette*. Instead of designing a single advertisement which covered the general advantages of their new product, they published all the pages of the instruction book over a consecutive eight week period. Phrases like; 'let it hang naturally, don't arrange it' and 'bring it forward without pause just short of the perpendicular' must have intrigued prospective buyers and guaranteed early sales. Common to all the ads was the line 'A Little Reel For Big Casts Ideal For Spinning, Float Fishing and Ledgering'.

My simplified version of the reel's instructions are as follows:

The cast is directly made from the forward-facing spool. This is swung into position on a notched aluminium leg which is held firm by a sprung ballbearing below the foot. After casting, the angler moves the spool to its secondary position, turns the rod on its side and operates the reel like a centre-pin. Line twist is overcome by reversing the spool. The handle will project from either side of the spool by simply releasing and relocking a spring clip.

Now, I hope you've got all of that 'cause I'll be asking questions later!

Only in America

I've always had a strange addiction to the more curious items of fishing tackle invented by eccentrics from around the British Isles. But nothing can prepare you for the truly bizarre curiosities found in the USA.

Our American cousins seem to excel in the production of items that range from the tasteless to the grotesque. The Miller Lite beer-can fishing reel, and the Harley Davidson telescopic rod and reel, housed in its own sheepskin-lined holster, are both worthy of a mention. But let's concentrate on the novelty lure market, for it is here that we find some of the more worrying examples found in American collections.

'The Georgia Cracker' bass bait is a wooden replica of a stick of dynamite! A green string fuse protrudes tantalisingly from its rear end, while two treble hooks hang in wait for a bass as the lure is drawn or bopped across the surface. I'm assured it gets a great reception from Georgia bass enthusiasts.

Moving on to something with a little more mechanical flair, I offer you the 'Gee Whizz' Action Frog. Patented in 1949, its cork body keeps it afloat, while its upturned hook makes it almost 'weed-less'. To give it its 'action', the angler pulls the line which causes its rubber legs to move forward on puppet-like strings. As the line is released, the legs flip back, and the frog shoots forwards!

And if you think that's extraordinary, marvel at the ingenuity of the Johnson 'Talking Frog'. Its voice is activated when two tiny contacts in its belly are connected by water. The instructions advise the angler that, 'Only 'Talking Frog' makes the sound of a distressed frog, and once in open water, bass will grab it!'

Before you get too caught up with the idea of frog fishing, I draw your attention to the 'Naked Lady' lure.

The early version of this delightful creature, patented in 1928, was in the form of a mermaid, but this later 'racier' model boasts hidden talents. Take her out

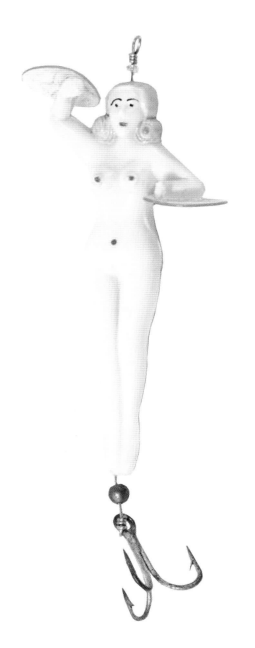

at night, shine a bright torch on her buttocks and breasts and '*voila!*' her parts shine with a luminous glow! It's been suggested, she'd be ideal for catching nocturnal sea trout.

Some years ago, I flew to the States for a meeting of the National Fishing Lure Collectors' Club (NFLCC) in Little Rock, Arkansas. A handful of British collectors also attended this five-hundred stall event, including the amiable Keith Elliot, angling correspondent for *The Independent.*

Keith isn't usually at his best early morning, but on the second day, shortly after breakfast, I found him beaming with barely concealed excitement. "Sit down and prepare yourself," he said, "I've found a real goody!" Expecting at least a glass-eyed, solid-silver British bait from before the turn of the last century, you can imagine my reaction when he handed me the unfortunately named 'Wanker' bass plug. Explaining that the bait was made in Japan by the Godagley company for the American market he added, "Isn't it great, neither nationality understands the word. Do you think it lost something in translation?"

Having found one item of 'naughty' tackle, our schoolboy sense of humour demanded that we now search for more.

tell you that political correctness prevails, as they are both known as 'Sambo' lures. The black gentleman is a diving bait and his white partner a surface lure. I'm sure the more curious among you will want to know what happens when you pull their barrels down. Well, how shall I put it? Their 'parts' spring to the upright position and, to settle any argument once and for all, there is no size differential!

Flying back to England and my comparatively sober tackle collection, a thought suddenly struck me. Keith is a dab hand at catching big pike on the Norfolk Broads. Supposing he landed a large fish on his ill-named bass plug, and the angler in a nearby boat called across, and asked what he was using . . . tricky!

The list of items to which American angling companies have attached sets of trebles, is almost endless. They include, miniature beer bottles and cans, false teeth, plastic cigars, lucky dice that revolve around a central wire and, secreted beneath a green baize modesty cloth, a miniature phallus! "No good to no one," shrieked the lady stall-keeper, greatly amused for the umpteenth time at her standard 'willy-under-the-cloth' joke!

It wasn't long before my eye fell on the two, barrel-clad plastic gentlemen you see in our other picture. I'm delighted to

Ooh . . . Matron!

I've had to send my cheque book to a convalescent home in Hove. Matron was furious! "Really Mr Sandford . . . this is not the first time is it? The poor thing is hanging in tatters . . . such abuse! Hopefully a good rest and some sea air should improve things!"

How does one explain to a member of the medical profession that one is cursed with the dreaded 'piscatoriana' and that cheque books, credit cards and all manner of savings are regularly abused to feed the craving?

I thought I'd been doing rather well over the last six months. The odd reel here . . . a lure there . . . nothing too extravagant. Then it happened! I was waiting in a Soho recording studio to do a voice-over (yes, I do take the odd day off from fishing!), when I was approached by a gentleman who asked if I was 'on the telly'. I was tempted to use the late Robert Morley's famous one-liner, 'No dear, you're mistaking me for a bowl of fruit!' but recognising a fellow angler I refrained and we chatted about my TV series *Just Fishin'* and finally got round to the subject of vintage tackle.

It transpired that at an auction in 1990 this gentleman had purchased the

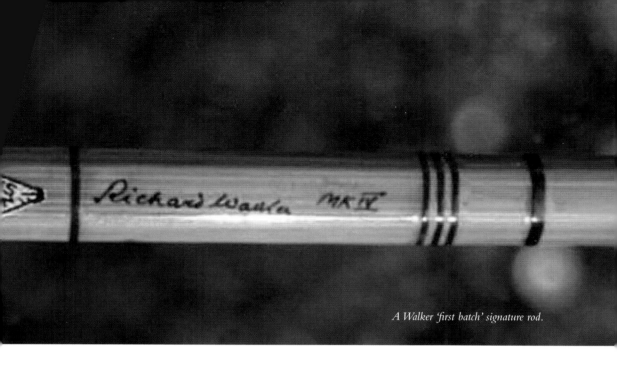

A Walker 'first batch' signature rod.

B. James Mk IV Avon rod that Richard Walker had allegedly presented to Bernard Venables. Now he had my undivided attention! He asked me if I knew anyone who might restore it to its former glory, as he had been fishing with it constantly for the past thirteen years! I told him I knew the only man who was capable of such a delicate task and the rod was duly delivered into my care.

It was not as bad as I had thought it might be. Water had got under most of the whippings and the top section wasn't straight. But my good friend Micky Wheeler is truly blessed with a great talent.

With equal amounts of skill and witch-craft he revitalised the whippings without having to replace them. Like a conjurer performing his best trick – one day the top section of the rod had a severe 'set' . . . the next day it did not! When the transformation was complete Micky asked me if the rod was to become part of my collection. I explained that it was not for sale but that I was still hopeful.

Within a week, email negotiations were underway and swiftly passed from 'no chance' to 'possibly' to 'how much?' Unfortunately, when I first saw the rod I was asked for a valuation and had told the truth! The owner now with one crippling stroke added 25 per cent to that figure to see if I was serious. Weeks passed until I finally decided that I had to own this piece of angling history. I dragged my cheque book screaming from the drawer, wrote as quickly as my trembling hand would allow and ran to the postbox. I walked home imagining that I could hear the late Richard Walker and Bernard Venables roaring with ghostly laughter.

The rod is signed by Bernard and inscribed in Indian ink, 'Richard Walker Mk IV Avon'. But is this Walker's writing? I don't think so!

The history of the Mk IV rod has been documented many times so I won't dwell on it here. Briefly, the facts are: in the late 1940s, Walker fished for carp with a cut down version of Allcock's famous 'Wallace Wizard'. This he found unsatisfactory and he experimented with various tapers with cane sent to him courtesy of Allcock and Co. The Mk II he considered to be too light. The 'double built' Mk III was too heavy, and he finally settled for the Mk IV with its 'through' action and stiff butt section.

He presented several of these rods to his fellow members in the Carp Catchers' Club including Denys Watkins-Pitchford ('BB') and Bernard Venables. In September 1952, commercial production of the rod was put in the capable hands of B. James of Ealing and in October of that year, Walker signed the first production run of approximately twenty-five rods to help promote its launch. It is thought that it was not until late 1953 that a transfer of Walker's signature was produced and applied to all new rods.

The success of the Mk IV was immediate so it is not unreasonable to assume that within months, it was no longer possible to supply rods with Walker's signature.

Over the last few years, at least eight early Mk IV carp and Avon rods have been discovered with details written in Indian ink along one of the hexagonal sides of the butt section. These, I believe, were inscribed in the shop when the signature rods were no longer available.

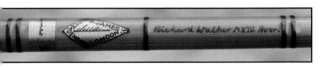

Two shop-inscribed rods

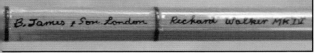

I recently put this theory to carp historian Chris Ball and he responded with a letter which reads in part, as follows:

'*I now think that a new classification is applicable in the evolution of James rods which were produced, and subsequently sold in the shop between late 1952 and early 1953.*

'*The evidence I've seen in recent years points towards a period of unprecedented demand following the "first batch" being sold. It isn't hard to understand why: Walker's record fish, adverts in* Angling Times, *etc.*

'*Though we know shop owner, "Jimmy" Bruce tried his hand at scrawling, "Richard Walker Mk IV Carp" or "Avon" along the butt (I have seen two examples), the "Built to Endure" Mk IV Avon you showed me has writing which is very similar to other rods of the same vintage that I've come across in the last few years.*

'*Our conversation on the subject seems to point towards someone else in the shop inscribing rods sold to the general public for a few short months before James got hold of the proper transfers.*'

To further excite Mk IV 'anoraks', the way to distinguish Walker's genuine signature from the shop-inscribed rods, is the old-fashioned way Walker wrote the letter 'r' at the end of his name. Whoever inscribed the shop rods used the more familiar version of the letter.

As I write, it is almost the end of February and Matron has just rung from Hove to say 'all is well'. I thanked her for her good works and added that the return of my cheque book would be just in time for the antique tackle auctions at Mullock Madeley in Ludlow and Angling Auctions in Chiswick. She was not amused!

The 'Venables Avon'.

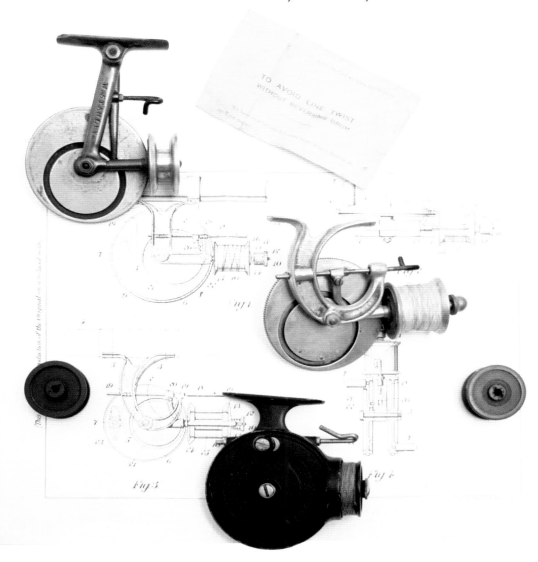

The story goes that when engineer Walter Stanley was repairing an Illingworth No.1 he had an idea for a more robust reel that would not be beyond the pocket of the average angler. He patented his brainchild in 1926 and christened it 'The Flyer Threadline' (middle right). The idea, like so many great innovations, was a simple one. As the angler turned the handle, the edge of the handle plate pressed against a washer on the back of the spool and a 'shepherd's crook' flyer, driven by an offset groove in the back of the plate, spread the line. (Are there any questions?!) He developed 'The Flyer' from a reel he made himself (top left) and supplied tackle shops on a sale or return basis. Sadly marketing was not Stanley's strong point but he did have the good sense to take his idea to Allcock & Co. in the early 1930s. They recognised the potential, redesigned the reel, and brought 'The Allcock–Stanley' to the market at the bargain price of 22/6d.

It was an immediate success and sold in its thousands. Although designed for light float fishing, reports of it landing large salmon and pike soon enhanced its reputation.

Stanley wrote to Allcock & Co early in his association with them complaining, 'I made a mistake in designing this reel. It had simplicity and a long life. The life of the reel was the whole fishing life of the angler. Bad for business!'

But it wasn't. Stanley's reel gave anglers the chance to fish with a fine line, on a reliable reel, sold at a competitive price. What a great epitaph!

LIGHT CASTING FOR ALL

(4th Edition)

THE HAND BOOK
OF THE
ALLCOCK-STANLEY
LIGHT CASTING REEL

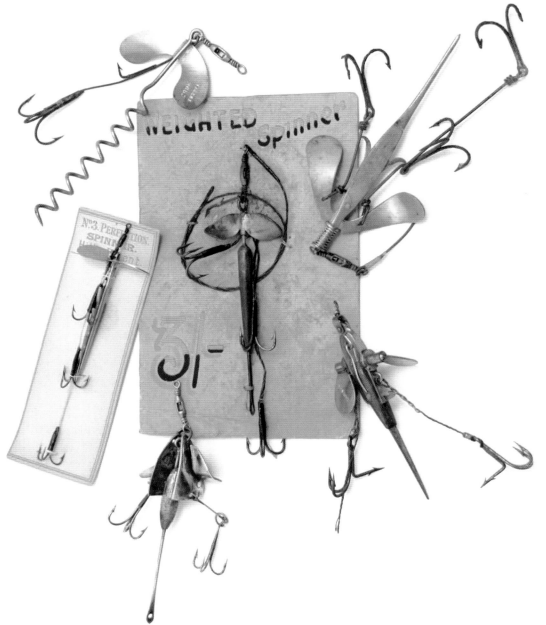

First Mount Your Bait

There seems to have been a flurry of activity around the turn of the century when the angling world decided that it was not sufficient to attach a live, or dead bait, to the end of your line with a simple hook. To stand any chance of securing a bite, the angler must now mount his bait on a complicated device with fins, flying trebles and a leaded body spike. Some baits even had to endure the indignity of wearing a small metal helmet not, as one might suppose, as a fashion accessory but as an aid to security.

The carded example in the centre of our shot is the standard pattern which dates from the early 1900s. I'm particularly fond of the artwork!

Top left, is Emerie's Corkscrew bait Mount, patented in 1892, yet another dual-purpose angling accessory. It's amazing the constant correlation that exists between angling and alcohol.

In 1891 Allcock & Co. seemed even more delighted with their Champion Spinner (next right). Having forced the apparatus down the fish's throat you wound the knurled disk at the head of the mount and two curved spikes emerged inside the bait to hold it firmly in place.

Below the Champion is the unbelievably rare Hardy Crocodile Spinner. Its adjustable fins allowed it to spin at various speeds and rotate in the opposite direction to avoid line twist.

Middle left on the small card is one of my favourites it was patented by James Hill, a lithographer from Liverpool, in 1895. He encouraged confidence in anglers by making the central blade plain on one side but with hooked serations on the other, so once the bait was mounted it stayed that way.

Finally, bottom centre, we find Allcock's A1 Spinner marketed in 1901. It has an adjustable metal helmet which according to the *Fishing Gazette* '. . . will fit any bait and protect it from being injured or destroyed by weeds, stones etc.'

There are many other examples which feature this kind of aquatic 'crash hat'. Some even required one to remove the fish's head entirely and fit it with a false one made of lead!

It's sad that our ancestors had to stoop to using these barbaric devices. It's even sadder that I seem to collect them!

Cabin Fever Cure

A grand piano stands in the main reception area of the Doubletree Hotel, Somerset, New Jersey, and one is welcomed on arrival with a selection of light classics. Faultless arpeggios and tiny glissandos embellish every phrase. I looked in vain for the pianist, expecting any moment, to see a 'Liberace' of diminished stature spring in to view. Sadly, this grand instrument turned out to be totally automatic.

I watched amazed, as the keys depressed and released themselves on exactly the right notes. This, of course, led to bad behaviour the following evening when leaving the bar! I was just in time to take up my position at the keyboard and, as I welcomed new arrivals, mime furiously to one of Scott Joplin's finest! My travelling companion, Neil Freeman, decided it was 'time for his walk'!

Towards the end of last year, we had both complained that 'cabin fever' was getting the better of us and it was time to get away. A three-day fly fishing show in the States seemed to be just the 'tonic' we were looking for . . . but, nothing had prepared us for the quality and size of this particular 'extravaganza'. As their publicity proudly announced: 'The Fly Fishing Show . . . now in its twelfth year . . . Fly Fishing is not part of the show, it *is* the show!'

The Garden State Exhibition Center next to the hotel is only just big enough to house over two hundred and fifty exhibitor booths, nearly fifty fly tyers and eleven thousand visitors over the three days. Our first stroll around the aisles took a little over two hours. If one needed a rest, then back in the hotel, every hour, on the hour, a choice of five one-hour talks on every subject from ice fishing to choosing the right hackle feather was on offer.

In the two larger seminar rooms, each capable of seating at least one hundred, lectures from 'notables' like A. K. Best were in full swing, eight times a day. Casting demonstrations, an author's booth - you name it, they had it, and all for a $12 entrance fee!

The US end of our trip was organised by the stunningly efficient Mrs Gerry Serviente. The hotel was comfortable, the food was fine, but I don't recommend the weather in New Jersey in January! It was so cold the Hudson froze over, and the ferries couldn't operate for two days. But don't be put off; this is a travelling show which appears at eight different locations including Colorado and California, so one can combine a visit to the show with sunnier pursuits and a bit of fishing.

On our second day, we spent time chatting with stallholders and watching demonstrations of every conceivable fly-fishing gadget and innovation. One of the biggest crowds accumulated around the Waterwisp stand. Their range of beautifully tied flies float with the hook on top rather than underneath. It's not a new idea but one they have refined, producing forty-seven different tyings in eight sizes down to size 22. The small flies shown on these pages are Waterwisp flies.

The show was not without its UK representatives, Steve Thornton amazed onlookers, as usual, with his extraordinary talent for tying realistic nymphs. The Americans had never seen anything quite like it and Steve's 'Flytyer's Masterclass' CD was selling well to those looking for a new challenge.

The busiest travel booth was manned by the Irish Tourist Board, with Jim Robinson and the crew dispensing wit and charm in all directions. How they managed to keep it up for three days is beyond me! Perhaps they have access to intravenous Guinness! It was ironic that we travelled all the way to the States only

to be reminded of the piscatorial delights on our own doorstep.

Anglers with a more 'traditional' approach to the sport were well catered for with specialist 'boutique' operations producing custom-made reels, luggage and, of course, cane rods. These, with their hand-engraved silver fittings and high lacquer finish, lay in slender, green-baize-lined mahogany cases. Bathed in light from a halogen heaven, their keepers spoke in hushed, reverential tones when discussing their merits. I'm afraid I got the giggles when told that when purchasing, I would be making the most important decision of my angling career. At around $3,000 it would also be the moment I went completely barking. Frankly, although these rods were aesthetically stunning, I didn't see anything that came up to the standard of our own Edward Barder.

On the stand of one internationally famous tackle company, I found a curious little sticker attached to all their current rods; it read, 'Warning - this product contains a chemical which is known in the state of California to cause cancer and birth defects'. Presumably, if you fish in any other states, you're OK!

Finally, the fly tyers. These guys are truly amazing. Positioned at high tables so that your eyes are in line with their hands as they work, they construct everything from a size 22 gnat, to salmon flies that sell for $350 for a single framed example. I don't remember how many hours I spent watching these artists at work but having recently decided to polish my own tying skills, it was both exhilarating and depressing. Examples of much of their work can be found in the magazine *The Art of Angling*. One rather startling salmon fly had been constructed, in the best possible taste, of course, to represent the 'Stars and Stripes'. Not to be out-tied, by our American cousins, I asked Alan Bithell to tie me a Union Jack mayfly for this chapter. Oh dear!

I shall visit the Fly Fishing Show again; not only because I need more than three days to take it all in, but because I can now mime faultlessly to 'the Moonlight Sonata' and it's a damned sight easier than Scott Joplin.

Spoon Fed !

In Tin Cup Lake in the heart of the Yukon wilderness, you can catch whitefish, grayling and lake trout. But when I was fishing there in late July 2004, you could also catch fire! It was the hottest summer for one hundred years and there were no less than one hundred and thirty forest fires raging across the region.

Having read Chris Tarrant's splendid article in *Waterlog* some months earlier, I'd rung him to confirm that this was a venue that I would enjoy. He suggested I book immediately for myself and 'Er Indoors. Sadly, my wife was busy, so I booked the single.

Including a three-hour delay at Heathrow, the journey from London to Vancouver, and then on to Whitehorse in the heart of the Yukon, took twenty-six hours! Next morning we boarded a Cessna single-engined float plane for the 350-mile final leg.

Even though small aircraft are not my favourite mode of transport, a bird's eye view of the lakes and mountains soon took my mind off the fact that we were defying gravity a mile or so above the earth. I was just getting comfortable with my surroundings when our pilot started an animated conversation with the pilot of another aircraft as to the best final approach to our destination. This was prompted by the fact that as we neared Tin Cup, we were met by a wall of smoke. After a hair-raising twenty minutes we finally found a clear passage between the mountains at the south end of the lake. As our floats touched the water, it crossed my mind that I had just experienced the ultimate cure for constipation!

We taxied across the water and eventually made out the red roofs of Tin Cup Wilderness Lodge which was to be our home for the next week. It accommodates up to ten guests and is run to perfection by Larry and Jose Nagy. Larry is a fascinating host. A geologist by profession, he has found gold deposits all over the world, the rights to which he has mostly sold on to big mining companies.

Back in the 1960s when he was a young student, he helped build a wilderness lodge from the ground up. When the project was finished he dreamt that one day, he would have a lodge of his own . . .

and Tin Cup is the fulfilment of that dream. His Dutch wife Jose is a professional chef and the food is the best I've ever experienced in a fishing lodge. The double chalet-style rooms are clean and comfortable with plenty of hot water and power showers.

For the first four days of our stay, we fished in a smoky fog. It was an eerie, but frankly boring experience. The only fish rising was the occasional one- to two-pound grayling. Whitefish were caught on buzzers and to catch a lake trout, one had to troll huge white streamers on fast-sinking lines. These fish averaged three to five pounds with the occasional six- to eight-pound specimen if you could be bothered to stick at it. The more stalwart members of our party resorted to casting their fast-sinking lines into the fog between 11pm and 3am. A few larger fish were landed but frankly, I hadn't travelled five thousand miles at considerable cost to have my beauty sleep disturbed!

On the morning of the fourth day, three firefighters arrived by helicopter and installed sprinklers around the lodge in case the wind increased and the nearest fire, only thirty miles away, decided to gallop towards us.

I was depressed. I asked Larry that afternoon where all the legendary giant lake trout were hiding. "C'mon," he said. "I'll show ya." We jumped into the nearest boat, motored down the lake for about a mile, switched on the fish finder, and there they were, in thirty to sixty feet of water.

Larry explained that most of them were sleeping. "When they're hungry," he said, "they float up towards the surface, eat a grayling or two, or maybe one of their own, sink back down and spend the next forty-eight hours digesting their meal. The only chance to catch one in this heat is to troll a big spoon at around fifty feet."

This was food for thought. According to the brochure, I was on a fly-fishing holiday and, traditionally, these huge fish could be taken on a large sedge fly, but the seasons had come early and the larger fish had now retreated to the depths. Suddenly the thought of hooking one of these monsters, regardless of the method, was very tempting. But the next day, everything changed, the wind blew from the south, the smoke cleared, the sun shone and we were all totally overcome by the beauty of this extraordinary location.

My boat partner was the photo-journalist Peter Gathercole. He's covered every kind of fly fishing in almost every part of the world. Having had some rain in the night, he suggested we go to the south end of the lake and fish where a creek funnelled cool water in from the surrounding mountains. We had one of the most exciting morning's fishing that I can remember. Lake trout to fifteen pounds that savaged our flies and put a frightening bend in our 9-weight rods. Peter got all the shots he needed, I got arm-ache, and we returned to the lodge tired but happy.

This was our last day and having landed at least ten fish that morning I was happy to sit on the balcony of the lodge and soak up the atmosphere, but Larry made me an offer I couldn't refuse. "Wanna try for a big one?" he said. Within moments we were trolling huge red and white spoons with single barbless hooks at around fifty feet. The fish finder beeped. "There they are," said Larry, "let's hope some of them are awake."

I won't give you the rod-arching, shoulder-aching, adrenalin-pumping ten paragraphs but suffice it to say that a huge lake trout of 27lb 6oz gave me an extremely hard time for about twenty minutes and thanks to Larry's expert direction, we eventually got the net under it!

Will I return to Tin Cup? You bet I will, but as Mr Tarrant suggested, next time I'll take 'Er Indoors because this is truly a family destination. Like any fishery anywhere in the world, you've got to 'catch it right', but in my opinion, the wildlife, the tranquillity and the warm welcome make Tin Cup one of the top ten fishing locations on the planet.

Cheeky Maggots !

Once upon a very, very, long time ago, when I was in my early teens, I used to cycle from Coulsdon in Surrey to fish the river Mole near Cobham. Today, I would think twice about doing the journey in the car, but in those days it was a great expedition. With sandwiches, lemonade and bait in my saddlebag, and Grandad's precious three-piece bamboo rod strapped to my crossbar, I hardly noticed the ped-alling - large chub were my only concern.

A recent addition to my tackle at the time was a maggot chute. I can't remem-ber how I came by it, but my much more practical toffee tin with punctured lid was relegated to 'refill' status. I thought the shoot was a marvellous device, and had no idea then that similar containers had been around since the turn of the century.

Arriving in Cobham very early one Sunday morning, I went in search of my friend Nobby Brown to show him this latest tackle innovation. Nobby was a few years older than me, and a most accom-plished angler, thanks mainly to his Dad, also called Nobby, who was the local match champion.

I found Nobby Junior landing a small dace in our usual swim. He was most impressed with my chute and suggested he might swap me a Dinky toy delivery van for it! I declined, and asked if we might show the chute to his Dad to get what amounted to a 'professional' opin-ion. "He'll not have time for that thing," said Nobby, "he stores his maggots in his cheek! Says it keeps 'em wet and warm so's they fish better!"

I didn't know whether to believe him or not. My mother certainly didn't when I told her. In fact, I was told not to be so revolting!

A few weeks passed, but the thought of Nobby's dad with a mouthful of maggots wouldn't leave me. I decided to ask one of the older club members if it was true. "Not any more," he said, "when he won the last match, the organiser slapped him on the back by way of congratulations, which caused him to swallow . . . he keeps them in his pocket now!"

Me and the Mrs ... Fishes ! - Nashville

In September last year, we took our fishing rods to Nashville, Tennessee, the country music capital of the world. Here, fishing for trout and bass, we found ourselves . . . flirting with the timber!

'You're the Reason Our Children are Ugly!' Gelly and I couldn't believe our ears, but there it was - another fine example of a tasteless and politically-incorrect country song that we could add to our ever expanding collection!

We'd flown to Nashville to fish for trout and the striped and small-mouth bass that inhabit the Cumberland and Caney Fork rivers.

Our Orvis-endorsed guide, Jay Clementi, had tuned the radio in his 4x4 to give us the best chance of adding to our 'tasteless titles' list. He gave us his dazzling American smile, consumed another mouthful of beef jerky and said, "I've just remembered another one - 'If it Ain't One Thing, it's Your Mother!'"

Unless you're steeped in local knowledge, you must have a guide on these mid-Tennessee rivers. They are both headed by hydro-electric dams and, unless you are familiar with the generating schedule, that beautiful fish-filled run you fished yesterday could, today, rise six vertical feet within an hour and leave you stranded! Jay told us he has a 'grid' of the river system in his head and, once he knows the schedules, he can always find somewhere to fish.

Sometimes we'd float the river for most of the day, stopping only occasionally. But, on low water days, we'd concentrate on two or three spots that were known to hold specimen fish.

This was our third day, and Gelly was keen to catch a striper. This beautiful fish is part of the bass family and usually found in salt water. But back in the 1960s, these local freshwater rivers had been stocked with the species to control the gizzard shad that were overpowering the local fish population.

On the first day, I'd managed to secure a couple of stripers once I'd got used to casting a 9-weight line with a 350 gramme sink tip and a fly called the Tennessee 'Half and Half'. This is half a Deceiver and half a Clouser minnow and though it's not unduly heavy, after you've been casting for an hour, in what was never less than 86 degrees of heat, the word 'shade' takes on a whole new meaning!

The method of fishing this fly was interesting; as the boat glided slowly downriver, Jay continually encouraged us to 'flirt with the timber'. This involves casting forward as close as you dare to any sunken tree or snag, letting the fly sink and, as you pass the spot, stripping in with a fast, jerky retrieve. Three short pulls, one long . . . three short pulls, one long . . . The take is heart-stopping; suddenly from nowhere, two, sometimes three, huge stripers chase the fly. One grabs it and immediately tries to get back into the snag. They are dogged fighters and as often as not will have you back in the timber before you know it. I'm proud to say, we never lost a fish but this was almost entirely due to Jay's expertise at getting the boat over the snag and holding it steady while we persuaded the fish to come out of hiding.

Gelly cast valiantly all that morning but it wasn't until just before lunch that she finally hooked an $8^{1}/_{2}$-pounder as it ambushed the fly from behind a submerged tree stump. To say she was thrilled is an understatement!

Lunch as always, appeared from Jay's cooler and we sat in the shade deciding where we might fish that afternoon. He explained that he knew a good trout spot downriver but, because the generated water had not yet reached us, we might have to 'walk' the boat down some of the shallows! This was no great hardship as the boat, a Gheenoe specially outfitted in Florida, and a cross between a canoe and a small flats skiff, is surprisingly light.

As we headed downriver the temperature rose high into the 90s and the water began to rise very slowly. I couldn't believe that trout would feed in the heat but Jay explained that the rising water comes from the bottom of the dam and is icy cold!

We must have caught twenty trout averaging around nine inches that afternoon. The method was a simple one; cast upstream and, as the fly lands, put a large mend in the line and feed line as the fly heads downstream. We used almost any small dry as an indicator with a Lightning Bug tied 'piggy back' to the rear of the hook and suspended about eighteen inches below. Once in every half-a-dozen takes, the trout would eat the fly, but mostly it was the bug.

As the day ended and the mist thickened over the water, it was comforting to know that there was an experienced hand on the tiller. The sunset was spectacular . . . heron and wild turkey rose through the mist and Gelly and I both

agreed that these waters, where we rarely saw another angler, were something very special.

Evening entertainment in the country-music capital of the world was not difficult to find. Whether taking your seat for a concert at the Grand Ole Opry, or taking a beer at one of the many smaller venues and bars, you are guaranteed a good time. Our favourite haunt was the Station Inn but rumour has it that this piece of Nashville's precious musical history is now under threat from developers. One can only hope it survives. We didn't hear any songs there to add to our politically incorrect list, but we did manage to cull a few titles from the local residents! Our favourites are: 'I Caught her Drinking Johnny Walker with Tom, Dick and Harry',' Don't Know Whether to Shoot Myself or Go Bowlin' . . . and, our special commendation for length was 'You can Take the Boy out of the Country, but You Can't Take the Bullets Outta that City Boy who just Cut me Off in His Saab!'.

On our last day, we decided to fish two tributaries, the South Harpeth river, and Tumbling Creek. Jay explained that we would catch mostly small fish but, there was always a chance of a 'big ol' Bass' if we waded quietly and once again, flirted with the timber. How right he was. In about eight feet of water on a sharp bend in the stream, the undercut bank was home to a tangle of waterlogged timber. "If you're gonna tempt 'em . . ." said Jay, "put on the 'Half and Half' and strip it fast past those snags." The result of this timely advice was a $3^1/_4$lb small mouth bass. Always listen to your guide!

It made a pleasant change to be wading all day in cool water, but next time, we'll dispense with the waders and 'wet wade' in boots and quick-dry trousers.

Beaver, raccoon and possum watched our progress up Tumbling Creek and, at one point, a stag decided to see how we were getting on.

The most successful fly of the day, was a tiny green 'Dayglo' popper. It never stopped catching fish: brown, rainbow and brook trout, more small-mouth bass, red-eye bass, long-ear sun fish (also known as 'pumpkin seeds'), and the most spirited takes of all were from blue gill. Jay assured us that two or three of these make a great meal: just de-scale, fillet and pan fry in flour and butter.

Fishing around Nashville is an experience we will definitely repeat but the toughest part of the trip was deciding which, out of around twenty contenders, should be our top three 'Tasteless Titles'. Many of course were unprintable but after hours of diligent deliberation, we finally chose the very best of a very bad bunch. so . . . may we offer in reverse order:

At *Number 3:*

'I Still Miss You Baby, but My Aim's Getting Better!'

At *Number 2:*

'I'd Rather Have a Bottle in Front of Me, Than a Frontal Lobotomy!'

And at *Number 1* . . . the winner is:

'Drop Kick Me Jesus Through the Goal Posts of Life!'

YEE-HA!

And here's how Gelly saw things:

Gellyvision

I'm often asked why I so enjoy our fishing adventures. I think it has a lot to do with experiencing the simple pleasures one remembers from childhood. Gliding slowly down a river on a beautiful day . . . being amongst the wildlife. Mind you, casting a heavy 9-weight line was a little daunting! My training as a classical dancer was a great help when I had to call on all my powers of balance, co-ordination and accuracy. It is not a skill that can be achieved when 'multi tasking'! It required all my concentration before I had that rewarding moment when Jay whispered, "Hey Gelly . . . good cast!" So, for once, I was with the boys, concentrating on only one thing at a time!

Top of my list on all these trips is comfort. Do we have sun lotion, bug repellant, enough water and snacks etc? Nashville is a great town for shopping! But it takes a little getting used to the fact that every other shop assistant seems to be a singer-songwriter waiting for their 'big break'! Even the guy in charge of fruit and veg. at the local Wild Oats store told us that after twenty-five years, he's still hoping for one of his songs to make it in the country charts!

Finally, as Chris has already indicated, 'If you want to get a fish, get a guide!' This old saying was never more apt than on Nashville's local rivers. Jay Clementi is skilful, helpful and patient and he provides a good lunch! I wouldn't hesitate to recommend him and, in case you're wondering, yes, he is also a singer-songwriter!

If size matters and big is beautiful, why aren't pike flies one of the great collectables? Probably because their appeal hovers somewhere between the sacred salmon fly and the common lure. Last year, I took a display of these flamboyant old stagers along to a local fly fishers gathering expecting that they would be the stars of the show. Not a bit of it! All they raised were a couple of sniggers and an enquiry as to whether I'd fancy another half of warm beer and a sausage on a stick!

Fishing for pike with a fly has recently been hailed as a great new way to angle for these mythical fish. In a way it's true. Technology has given us the materials to cast a heavy fly in roughly the same way as we would when fishing for trout or salmon. But in 1876 *The Modern Angler* by 'Otter' tells us:

' . . . *in lakes or large rivers a colossal artificial Dragon fly with two large hooks at the tail and another concealed in the wings will be found a first rate bait for large Pike. It is to be used somewhat like a spinning bait, but without any weight on the line, and is to be worked on or near the top of the water'.*

I believe this is what our American cousins call 'a skittering bait' so it is not strictly a 'fly' in the purest sense. Frankly, I don't care! I think they are important, and have searched out a dozen or so in the last decade, all in various stages of decay. The remains found on an old hook will usually give you a clear idea of the original pattern. Luckily, fly tyer and photographer Terry Griffiths is a good friend of mine and an expert at sympathetic restoration. He has also managed to accumulate many of the rare materials needed for this type of work.

Mind you, restoration of any kind is frowned upon by a considerable section of the collecting community. My attitude is, that if I could afford to collect vintage cars and found a 1928 Bentley which had had an argument with a lamp-post, I wouldn't drive it around showing off the damage!

I'm not interested in tatty remains. Big or small let it be beautiful again!

Pike fly before (above) and after (below) restoration.

Too Good to Fish With

Fishing with Peter Drennan is a wonder-fully ordered experience. Once advised on the float, the line and exact shotting to suit the species and conditions, there is absolutely no doubt that you will catch.

It's just a question of how many.

I've had the good fortune to fish along-side some brilliant anglers: John Wilson, Bob James, Keith Arthur and Peter Cockwill to mention but a few, and although Peter Drennan would vehemently deny that he falls into this heady category, believe me, he does! To say he avoids profile-enhancing moments is an understatement. How I persuaded him to appear in the first show of my television series *Just Fishin'* is still a mystery. Even though you may not be aware of Peter's angling skills, step into any fishing shop in the UK and many in Europe, and you will without doubt become aware of his surname on a vast array of angling-related products.

Towards the end of last season, Peter and I both agreed we needed a day off and repaired to his local river to see if there was anyone 'at home'. We got chatting about how he'd made his first float when he was eleven, and then in 1964 how he'd entered some hand-crafted examples into a competition in *Fishing* magazine and won joint first prize.

Richard Walker was one of the judges and remarked, "They are almost too good to fish with . . . I'd be afraid of losing them."

Such praise encouraged Peter to offer his floats for sale at local tackle shops, and now, nearly forty years later, he's still coming up with ideas that make angling a more enjoyable experience.

We'd been fishing for about an hour when I managed to catch a reasonable chub on the 'lead'. As I returned the fish to the water Peter said, "Did I ever tell you about the railway chub?"

"No," I said.

"Ah well . . ." he said. "Pour us another cup of tea and I will . . ." And he did!

When Peter gets that faraway look in his eye, you just know it's going to be 'a good 'un!' He had a sip of tea and said:

"These big chub lived right underneath a railway bridge which only cleared the water by a few feet. The only way to get a bait right under and down to the fish was to cast diagonally across the river towards the bridge on a very light, critically balanced link ledger, drop a big loop of line into the current and use it to pull the link round in a big arc. This way you could get a bait three or four yards under the bridge where the chub felt confident.

"Of course it was the late, great Peter Stone who popularised the link ledger and taught me at first hand its subtleties and refinements. This was back in the late 1950s when he was already a grand master and I was just a kid. Back in those days, the tackle shops didn't offer the sheer range of equipment which is now available. But I was good with my hands and I could make things. I made rods, moulded leads, knitted nets, rod rests, feeders and of course floats.

"I received a lot of encouragement not only from Stoney but also from Dick Walker and the Taylor brothers with whom I was fortunate enough to be fishing. But the real incentive was that some of the items actually helped us to catch more fish. The feeders and the floats were a particular success, making a tangible difference to our catches.

"Some of the float designs were tried and discarded, others proved really successful. Some became classic fish catching systems, like the Driftbeater with its critically buoyant sight bob at the end of a long antenna, which for us revolutionised lift-method fishing. It was so exciting to be involved in the development of new methods and their step by step progression with the floats themselves.

"I was particularly enthusiastic about my flat stret-pegging vanes which took a lot of shot but presented a small surface area to the current. On a tight line I could work these harp shaped floats out into the flow, then back in towards an undercut bank, catching fish as the bait washed right in against small ledges. Although highly effective, it was a system that never really caught on but it's gratifying that forty years later, the flat lollipop float uses exactly the same principle and is now recognised as a deadly method on the pole.

"Of course I don't want to make it all sound too vocational or reverential. It was certainly never that! The driving force, the compulsion, was to catch fish and the process was always fun. Stoney, God bless him, had that lovely character which could handle being the fall-guy of our group; he was the target of Walker's sharp wit, Ken and Joe Taylor's piss-taking and the practical jokes of us kids. Stoney, being that much older and dedicated to the pursuit of big fish, he would often give us a bollocking for messing about and not taking it seriously.

"On our annual pilgrimage to the Royalty, myself and Ian Tolpott had received a right 'telling off' from Stoney for wasting our time down on Christchurch Beach with girls when the barbel were going. We always stayed at Bill Warren's guest house because he was the top man on the Hampshire Avon at the time. Stoney's dressing down happened to coincide with a request from Mrs Warren that I sort out our spare tackle in the garage, because something in there smelt really awful.

"*I found the offending item to be a newspaper parcel of putrefying mackerel which had been on a sea-fishing trip with us out of Mudeford the previous week and which were now in a nice liquified state, held together only by damp newspaper. Stoney and Joe Taylor were off down the Royalty with a gallon of maggot, whereas Ian and I were back off down the beach in pursuit of the girls.*

"*They were about to leave with a slightly self-righteous air, and I only just had time to slip the parcel of mackerel under the driver's seat of Stoney's new Minor 1000 Traveller before they set off.*

"*It transpired that they had to have all the car windows open on the way down to the Royalty and Joe concluded that they were the stinkiest fish maggots he'd ever encountered. Unfortunately during their six- or seven-hour session they left the car in the Royalty car park, windows closed, liquid mackerel broiling nicely in the hot summer sun.*

"*On their return, they opened the doors and the stench was overwhelming. Joe said it cleared the Royalty car park in minutes.*

"*Stoney eventually forgave us. Even though the windows on his car had to stay open on every trip for weeks afterwards. Criminal, really.*

"*I'm very fortunate that after all these years, I'm still animated by new methods and the development of new items of tackle. The driving force remains the same - to catch more and better fish, although it's perhaps not quite as much fun without 'The Stone'.*"

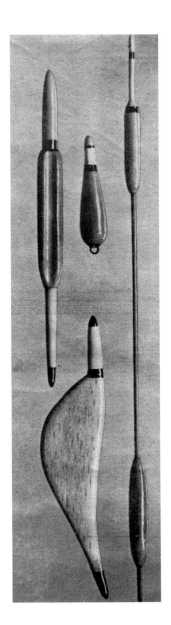

I don't remember what else we caught that day but I do remember asking Peter Drennan how he would sum up his feelings for the humble float. "Well," he said, "I think H. T. Sheringham got it right in his book *An Angler's Hours* when he wrote, 'There is only one thing more pleasing in appearance than a float and that is its disappearance'.

The
Golden Toast
Awards

I don't think I've ever given a public airing to my toast 'rant'. You see, I love toast, but it's got to be 'just right' . . . it can be white or brown, I don't mind, but as self proclaimed 'Toast Master', white bread, toasted golden brown, would probably get my highest marks.

Over the last few years, lack of international attention to this most important of breakfast ingredients has become apparent because, my wife and I are unashamed 'foodies' travelling miles in search of culinary excellence.

'Spume of lark's tongues on a bed of morning plucked elves' toes'? . . . Why not? 'Lightly broiled vole's liver garnished with a fricassee of dandelion petals'? . . . Yes, certainly!

But, what we have found is that no matter how many Michelin stars an establishment boasts, no matter how controversial a chef's behaviour, come breakfast time, that simple essential which guarantees a good start to the day will be ruined!

Can anyone tell me which culinary dictat decreed that as soon as you've ordered the beverage of your choice, a rack of limp underdone 'sadness' is placed in front of you? This is especially annoying if you've just ordered a cooked breakfast. "May I please have my toast with my eggs and bacon?" The question hangs in the air, and usually brings the dining-room to a complete standstill; rather like Oliver Twist asking for 'more'. The breakfast waiter, hardly able to believe his ears, returns to the table and peers quizzically at the lacklustre slices he has just placed before me. "Yes," I say, "I would like my toast with my cooked breakfast. These pallid slices are already cold and frankly, they have not had an intimate relationship with your toaster!" He removes the offending slices and bristles away to the kitchen. Eventually, the eggs and bacon arrive but what now occupies the toast rack looks like a souvenir from Hiroshima!

It's not only the UK that fails the 'toast test' . . . at Little Palm Island, off the Florida Keys, our breakfast waitress made an almost tearful confession: "I'm so sorry, the toast is only done on one side. It's because only one side of the toaster is working." My wife and I thought for one moment we might be on US 'Candid Camera' . . . but no . . . not a lens to be seen. I beckoned the waitress closer and muttered in my best 'confidential' tone, "Toast one side, turn the bread around and then toast the other." The light dawned. She sped away returning moments later with the hot golden slices and, with a smile like a razor said, "Enjoy!"

At Marfield House in Corey, Co. Wexford, they have the good sense not to make the clientele's toast. Every breakfast table boasts its own toaster and you are presented with a basket of fresh brown and white bread so fussy buggers like me can toast away to their heart's content!

Perhaps the only way to raise the profile of toast in the consciousness of the world's hoteliers, is to initiate the 'International Golden Toast Awards'. Hosted by Des O' Connor at the Albert Hall, a bevy of scantily clad beauties could present bronze, silver and gold toast racks to the deserving winners!

But, what's toast got to do with fishing you may ask? A secret bait perhaps? No, apart from the traffic, toast was the only failure of our trip to this year's Game Fair. With dogged determination, we drove the four and a half hours from West Sussex to Yorkshire, (Incidentally, if anyone should ever ask you if you'd like to go to Harrogate during Game Fair weekend, there is a five word question it would pay you to memorise: 'What time is the helicopter?')

Having scrutinised the local hostelry guide, we decided to stay at the Devonshire Country House Hotel and it turned out to be a great find: comfortable rooms, super food and a wine list that would be hard to beat anywhere in the UK. My wife even booked in for a facial and returned refreshed and looking ten years younger!

However, breakfast had its usual toast 'fault'. The barely warm slices were delivered as we poured our first cup of tea, but they had something about them that I couldn't quite fathom. Closer inspection revealed a variation on the 'barely brown' category that one has come to expect. These slices were toasted all around the edges but not in the middle. I was so occupied trying to work out how this had been achieved that I forgot to complain! My eggs and bacon were spectacular and my wife proclaimed her haddock to be excellent!

The Game Fair was as we have come to expect. The two-hour queue to get in, the fifteen-minute walk from the car park and almost more dogs than people! I suppose one should be thankful that toilets are provided for the human attendees! Treading carefully down towards Fisherman's Row, past the helicopter rides, the all-terrain vehicle demos and the self-assembly jungle huts which instantly turn your back garden into a safari park, we came upon Paul Morgan doing a roaring trade on the Coch-y-Bonddu stand. Next door, our ebullient

Waterlog Editor was dispensing wit, charm and the latest offering from Medlar: *Great Pike Stories* by Fred Buller. I so enjoyed the first chapter that I've decided to save the remainder for those long winter evenings. It's great to see Fred in print again.

As for the Game Fair, I think our next visit will be when it returns to the South. We may still have to queue to get in, we may still have to park miles from the Fair, but at least we'll be able to start from home where, I can assure you, the toast is excellent!

Beautiful
Backsides

Vintage Tackle Tips No. 1: How to Ruin a Reel

Strip off every vestige of original patina. Coat with high gloss polyurethane varnish. Buff brasswork to a blinding finish. Now arm yourself with a handkerchief because when you discover you have not restored the reel but reduced its value by at least 60 per cent you're going to feel very sad!

Renovation is an art; an expertise achieved by those with a burning desire to return precious old tackle to its former glory. Some collectors are adamant that any collectable item be left in the condition in which it is found. Not subscribing to this 'junky' mentality, I like my 'stuff' to be tastefully 'brought forward'.

The three reels shown (left) are good examples of this persuasion. There was nothing drastically wrong with any of them. A rusty check spring here, a seized spool release there. But now they are back from the 'hospital' and feel very much at home with the rest of my 'beautiful backsides'!

Wood is affected more by atmospheric change than any other material used in the assembly of reels. Early makers used a 'strap' or 'spine' to accommodate the foot, and also to help stop the backplate from warping. This didn't always prove satisfactory, so the 'cross' or 'starback'

became the 'norm'. The Millwards 'frog-back' (far left), and the Allcock 'circle-back' (top left) are both old sea reels and required extra strengthening against attack by salt water.

Eventually, makers reinforced the back-plates of their sea reels by lining them with brass. David Slater of Newark found a novel way of showing off this feature with his 'segmented' or 'quadrantback' (bottom left), which was retailed through Carter & Co. circa 1910.

I think 'woods', as they are known in collecting circles, are important. Especially those that are named and also feature interesting metalwork.

But let's move on . . .

Vintage Tackle Tips No. 2: How to Ruin a Cane Rod

Remove rings and strip to the bare wood . . .

My favourite 'frontside' - the spectacular Bicycle Bell Alarm Reel!

A Magnificent Seven

I'm usually better known for my lure collection than my love of old angling books, but I couldn't resist showing you these little masterpieces of the publishers' art! With some fantastic collections recently coming on to the market there has never been a better time to get interested in books, though none of the little gems shown here has ever been seen before.

All of these very rare copies have come my way by various means, though you'd have to get up very early in the morning if you want to get hold of such beauties! But books like these are still out there.

To finish I'll give you a little teaser - I've heard of a book about bream angling written by none other than the doyen of trout fishers, Halford. I'm on the case, but not very near!

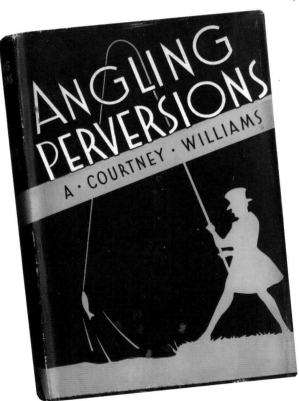

This is the original title of Courtney-Williams' classic, and needs no further comment, other than to say that the original print run of ten thousand copies was pulped before getting in to the bookshops. Some copies were thought to have survived the purge, but this is the only one known to be still in existence.

Copy in the Whitehouse Collection.

Another book doomed to failure from the start. After the roaring success of the 'How to Catch Them' series, Herbert Jenkins was taken in by a very plausible Scot, Angus McCoatup, writing under the name of 'Seangler'. Angus convinced the obviously senile senior editor to commission a whole range of fish-naming books. Both men were committed in 1957 after the first book was proofed.

Publisher's proof - only one copy known.

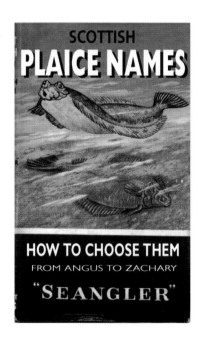

Hancock battled long and hard with his publisher Brian Rick to get his seminal work *Rod in Hand* published as *Hod in Hand*. Although Hancock was a bricklayer, and a very good one, he failed to convince Rick that the title would sell.

Publisher's proof - only one copy known.

This brilliant book, eventually published as *The Guileless Trout* caused a serious rift between coarse and game anglers in the early Fifties. McCaskie, in reality a brilliant bream angler who hated trout, was finally forced into a change of title by a High Court writ paid for by various private trout-fishing clubs and societies, determined to defend the honour of their favourite quarry

Copy from Sir Derek Strangeley-Brown QC - only one known.

Even in the non PC 1950s, this title was swiftly withdrawn by Herbert Jenkins before publication. Although a huge market existed in Canada (and probably still does) Jenkins still scrapped the project. Young went on to write the very successful, if less controversial *Sea Angling*.

Publisher's sample - only one copy known.

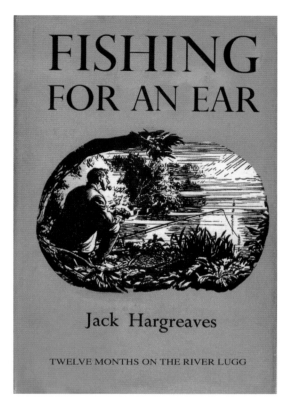

FISHING FOR AN EAR

Jack Hargreaves

TWELVE MONTHS ON THE RIVER LUGG

Loved for his wicked sense of humour, Jack Hargreaves had this dummy cover made for an awards presentation to the Ludlow AA in 1951.

Writer's copy - only one known.

Known affectionately as a 'bit of a looney' by his editor, Herbert Palmer nevertheless was a good writer, and *The Roving Angler* was undoubtedly his best book. This spoof copy was circulating around the publisher's office before being thrown away.

Copy rescued from a skip - the only one known.

THE RAVING ANGLER

HERBERT E. PALMER

It will not surprise regular Waterlog *readers to know that the computer skills and wit of Jon Ward-Allen had more than a little to do with this fine list of collectable angling literature.*

Eccentricity is found in many forms, but none stranger than the collector with a passion for ancient soft rubber products that will inevitably perish, harden and eventually turn to dust!

A good friend of mine has just paid £165 for the example shown above. But far be it for me to point the finger. There is a corner of my collection that houses almost every conceivable imitation of creatures that fish like to eat. A floating wooden bumble bee, caterpillars with bodies adorned with tiny shiny beads, several sizes of grasshopper, ladybirds and

128

beetles, bluebottles and house flies; in fact bugs and grubs of every description including an Indian-rubber worm patented by Morris Carswell on 8th April, 1883.

Carswell's Glasgow-based tackle business supplied the wholesale and retail trade from 1865 to the late 1920s and virtually cornered the market in artificial baits.

I once expounded in *Waterlog* on the joys of catching leopard trout in Alaska with mice tied from deer hair. But there is little new in angling: Carswell patented a mouse (shown below right) as early as 1926. His catalogue of that year tells us: '*This clever imitation is made of soft rubber, covered with real fur and is a splendid bait for Black Bass, Pike . . . per dozen 18/9.*'

An innovative thinker, Carswell also patented a method of concealing a swivel in the nose of a Phantom Minnow, a tackle case for holding rigged Phantoms, a method for straightening silk worm gut, a reel brake, a modified version of the famous Illingworth No. 2 threadline reel and a fly book.

One of his most successful imitation baits was the hollow, soft rubber Meadow Frog which floated on the surface and could be 'twitched' enticingly around the lily pads driving pike into a feeding frenzy. His strong porpoise-hide Phantom Minnows and his virtually indestructable 'horn' Minnows proved equally popular.

There are still a number of Carswell's moulded rubber baits that I've yet to discover intact. For example, there's no sign of his creepy Stone Catfish; and his Dragonflies in sizes 3, 4 and 5 inches prove equally elusive. And no one dare mention his rather sinister soft rubber crab!

Searching with great care through old tackle boxes sometimes has its rewards but it is rare to find examples in good condition. The word 'rubber' usually signifies flexibility but don't you believe it! One careless knock and you end up with a pile of bits and an old hook!

If you are the proud owner of a carded selection of these antique baits, please treat them with care. As any fetishist will tell you, old rubber can be a little unstable!

Collecting vintage fishing tackle is a game of highs and lows: great excitement when one finds that obscure and rare reel, and stultifying misery when one comes across a scarce item that is so badly distressed through lack of care, that the finest restorer in the land would only shake his head as he dropped it in the bin.

Rods rotten with worm and damp. Reels warped beyond any possible use. Flies 'mothed' so badly, that only the vaguest remnant of the original tying remains. I've seen cased fish that look as if they have been recovered from a nuclear holocaust. Creels that crumble to dust, because they once supplied a million termites with a hearty meal. Priceless brass reels, that have been dropped and bent. And metal tackle boxes rusted beyond use.

It is not as if anglers lack instruction on how to care for their tackle. How many times have you seen that 'Let's get our gear ready for the new season' article? With monotonous regularity, we are advised to administer a drop of oil here, and a squirt of WD40 there. We are urged to check our rod rings for grooves, and our fly boxes for bugs. Lovers of cane are told to rub down and re-varnish their rods and if, perish the thought, the top section should have taken a 'set', expert advice suggests that one either learns to fish around corners or reverses the rod rings so that the offending section flexes in the opposite direction.

If our forefathers had received such clear-cut advice, I wonder if more of their tackle would have survived. Searching through our ancient angling literature, it would appear that tackle maintenance was closely acquainted with witchcraft! Much of it is preposterous and beyond belief! The book I would recommend that gives a more than clear picture of how tackle was cared for with materials available at the time is, Frederick G. Shad's privately published work *A Concise Treatise on the Devices for Taking of Fish by the Means of Fly Fishing and the Methodical Maintenance of those Devices Through all Seasons. Accompanied by a Quaint Discourse on the Preparation of Edible Species as Tested by the Experience of Thirty Years.*

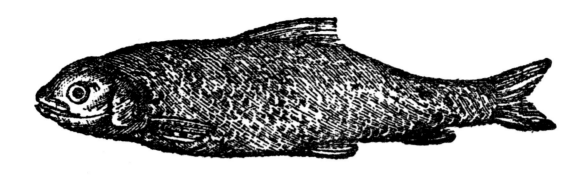

To quote the original text would require the reader to be well versed in old English, so I have taken the liberty here of using parts of Geoffrey Barn-Cruikshank's translation and inter-pretation (1928) also published privately.

On the matter of rod maintenance, Shad suggests that '*Thy rod, when inclement weather does cause the timbers to moan, should be laid on a bed of blighted hawthorn and doused throughout one day and one night with oil of Bog Weevil. Thereafter, caressed with fine silken cloth and left to settle in airy surroundings.*'

On reels, his advice is even more mys-terious: '*If a wynder be your pleasure, then at the fullest of the moon, remove your line and place your wynder in a small badger's bladder which has been dried and soaked in warm neck oil. Your line should be renewed with plaited horse hair and a fair haired maiden's tresses.*'

Shad makes no attempt to explain how to obtain these ingredients, presumably the 'fair haired maiden' lived nearby and didn't mind having her hair cut!

On artificial minnows, he refers to Walton's *Compleat Angler* and agrees that they are best made of 'sad French green silk', but goes on to suggest: '*Once a maker is found to assemble such an artificial minnow to your satisfaction, be sure to have about your person, at least one dozen examples. At the first sign of snow, wrap each one in the silver skin from the belly of a mackerel and place them, head to tail in a box of thin larch wood anointed with the flume of toad bile.*'

If you had the stomach for further tackle maintenance he suggested that flies *'that are crusted and stuck with the glue of use'* should be *'held in the grip of long tongs over a steaming cauldron of rosehip water, to which has been added a measure of sheep's blood'*.

If you consider this advice to be of a somewhat eccentric nature, his discourse on the preparation of edible fish pushes the credibility of his suggestions even further.

On the preparation of chub, he suggests that *'as Winter affords us little sport, and even less to adorn the table, be thankful therefore, if a Chub should come to your net. Dispatch him sharply and while still warm, set aside his innards.*

with the entrails in liberal quantity and bind to it the Chub with lengths of Rosemary. Within the cavity of the fish, place four dried newts, a plover's egg and a smear of vole paste.

'Allow all to cook slowly all day in Birch embers. When all is done, remove the Chub, and, with every ounce of strength at your command, throw it from you as far as you might. Now, all is ready, pour yourself a large measure of ale and eat the Elder branch.'

'Cut a branch of Elder that should be trimmed to the length of the fish, and planed flat on both sides. Anoint the Elder branch

Excerpts from Shad's Concise Treatise *are reproduced with kind permission from the Snell & Fador Angling Trust.*

133

Carp, Trout and a Bridge Too Far

July 2007 was an 'interesting' month, and it divided itself into three very distinct occasions: a bum-numbing blank on the first day of the coarse season; a picnic on the river Test that resulted in a 4lb brown trout caught with the help of a chum up a tree and a French fishing trip that produced an extra three pounds of body weight, a tiger trout and what can only be described as a 'bridge too far'.

Carp

For the past twenty years, June 16th has found me on a deep bend on the banks of the river Avon hoping for a large carp. The one exception was 2001 when my bride decided that that was the day we should be married! This year I believe that the only carp caught on the seven miles of our syndicate water, was by my chum John Knott, who hadn't held a coarse rod for over thirty years. He fished with a homemade Mk IV and a Hardy Altex that did impressions of a broken coffee grinder. The fish weighed about eight pounds and was caught ten yards from where I was sitting with my state-of-the-art carping equipment. I've asked John to find his own swim next year!

Trout

I'm rather keen on the gentle art of the angling picnic, and I don't mean two dodgy sandwiches grabbed from the nearest service station! For the past six years, our summer venue for the 'Sandford Piscatorial Picnic' has been Robin Elwes's stretch of the river Test above Mottisfont. Robin runs this syndicated water with his cousin William, and is kind enough to keep a few days avail-able for friends. Especially friends who lay on a three-course lunch, chilled champagne and a hot Kelly kettle!

Two days before the event, my wife Gelly goes into shopping overdrive. Then, stooped under the burden of freezer boxes, two rain-cover pavilions (just in case!) and enough fishing equip-ment to furnish a small shop, we engage four-wheel drive and make our way to the riverbank.

This year we were blessed with one of the few sunny days in June. The fishing was good, the lunch as ever was spectac-ular and after coffee we all pretended to read the Sunday papers whilst quietly nodding off!

Robin Elwes is tackle consultant and casting instructor for Farlows and Sportfish and some years ago had the doubtful privilege of teaching me to cast with a salmon rod. After tea on that sunny Sunday he found me staring glumly into my fly box. I complained that I couldn't find anything to tempt several large brown trout that I could see mov-ing in and out from under a nearby tree.

"They're a little skittish," he informed me. "And rarely take a dry . . . Come with me."

I cast with my left hand so that stand-ing on the left-hand side of the tree trunk, I had an easy cast upstream. "Show me your bugs," he said. I opened my fly box. "Good grief," he muttered. "Do you have anything a little more realistic?" I opened my other box. "Ah . . . that'll do . . . hang on a minute and when I tell you, cast out twenty feet."

With that he scrambled up the tree and gazed down into the water.

"There's a very nice one right under this branch I'm standing on. Cast out twenty feet and let the fly swing under the tree . . . no, that's twelve feet. Try again . . . no that's twenty-five feet . . . that's better . . . let it swing . . . twitch it . . . not so fast. OK . . . re-cast . . . "

This went on for about ten minutes with two changes of fly but eventually Robin shouted, "That's it!" . . . and it was! A very nice brown just over four pounds.

I think everyone caught that afternoon except one guest who said he'd had a wonderful time sleeping under the *Sunday Telegraph*. Long live the angling picnic!

More Trout (Tiger)

'Les Fontaines' Pacours de Pêche in the Isère region of France lies approximately equidistant within the triangle of Lyon, Valance and Grenoble. Its waters are supplied from local springs and the river Oron. In the centre of the fishery are two lakes, but the unique feature of this fishery, is that two streams circle the lakes in opposite directions. In places the path between the streams is so narrow I had the novel opportunity of casting upstream on both waters by simply turning around!

Local guide Patrick Chambert, was more than helpful with his advice and his hand-tied flies, one of which caught me my first tiger trout.

My good friend David Mindel had suggested that we try the fishery but was also keen that we experience the local menu at our overnight accommodation 'Ma Petite Auberge' in Pajay, five minutes from the fishery.

That evening we ordered the speciality of the house: deep-fried and battered baby trout that were no bigger than one's little finger. Between four of us, we ate two large dishes of these delicacies and to make sure we had difficulty rising from the table, they were accompanied by the finest gratin dauphinoise that I have ever tasted. These, along with far too many bottles of Côte de Rhône, made for one of the most delicious and reasonably priced meals that we have ever eaten in France.

A Bridge too Far

The next day, we travelled south to visit my son Jamie and his wife Greca, who live in Puivert which is about an hour from Carcassone. They dropped out of the London rat race just over a year ago, and are now the editors of *French Entrée Languedoc* which is the online resource for property, holidays and life in the Languedoc Roussillon. They had arranged for us to stay in a nearby village of Sonnac-sur-l'Eglise at, 'Le Tresor', a wonderful *chambre d'hotes* that has just received its first Michelin entry and is run by a British couple, Tilly and William Howard. If you are travelling in the area we guarantee you'll love it!

The village of Puivert is built either side of a gorge, along the bottom of which, runs the river Blau. As one crosses the bridge one can't help but notice, at the centre of its span, two small sheds nestling side by side. They were locked, and not without good reason. I asked my son if they were perhaps fishing huts. He

explained that nearly a hundred years ago, before indoor plumbing became fashionable, this was where the villagers lined up to answer the call of nature! Occupants obviously needed a head for heights, as the drop to the river below is about eighty feet.

Neither history nor the local tourist guide relates the internal design of this facility but knowing the French I wouldn't mind betting that the seating arrangement was nothing more than a plank with a hole in it!

Presumably, a discreet distance from the bridge there was a notice advising anglers to fish upstream!

The Ladies' Advantage

I don't remember when I first read about Miss Ballantyne's record 64lb salmon that she caught on the Tay in 1922, but I do remember thinking, 'Good for her. Everyone needs a bit of luck!'

Over the years, I've read most of the theories about why lady anglers catch bigger and better fish than us chaps. Frankly, I dismissed these scribblings as a series of poor excuses invented by men who wanted to prove that they were at an unfair disadvantage, when outfished by

the fairer sex . . . Akin to some new kind of bait mix or mystical fly, how could they possibly compete if they were lacking this mysterious ingredient? If I'd had the sense to pay a little more attention to detail, I would have realised that this research was, in fact, based on an irrevocable truth.

Nearly twenty years ago I met Gelly, the lady who is now my wife. I was attracted to her for all the obvious reasons but I soon discovered a bonus benefit . . . she was about to produce John Wilson's first fishing series being filmed around the world!

Naturally I asked permission to tag along, but was told firmly but with a smile, "No darling . . . I'm working!" Undeterred, I took her to a private carp lake in the hope that my skills as an angler might impress, and that I would be recognised as the ideal companion to accompany her on this worldwide trip. I explained the intricacies of the fixed-spool reel, showed her how to rig the bait and even allowed her to cast her own rod. It wasn't the greatest cast but it didn't go into the bushes on the opposite bank or fall on the ground behind her!

I was answering the call of nature about an hour later, when I heard the bite-alarm and Gelly's call, "It's all right darling. I've

got it!" When I returned she was in the water wearing my waders and giving considerable sidestrain to a carp that weighed in at 17lb. The first of four that day!

I didn't accompany her on her shoot, but since that outing we have fished together whenever we can and organise our own 'round the world' fishing adventures. Our holidays are the best of times and until recently I have chosen to ignore the fact that my wife usually catches the biggest fish. There was the 80lb tarpon and the 60lb cobia in Florida. The 8lb bonefish in the Caribbean. The enormous ray, and the shark that took nearly an hour to bring to the boat. I would always offer my congratulations but still secretly believed that these catches were more to do with luck and the skill of the guide. Undoubtedly these were contributing factors, but it was not until a couple of years ago when Gelly decided to take up the fly rod that I started to have my suspicions that all that research into what we'll call the 'Ladies' Advantage' might have some merit.

We had been invited to spend a day on the river Itchen and, towards the end of the morning, I was proudly having my photograph taken with a brown trout of just under four pounds that I had caught on a nymph. I was convinced that it would be the fish of the day. Not a chance! Gelly appeared with a fish of 4lb 2oz! I've now had that fish set up in a bow-fronted glass case. It gazes down on our dining-table as a constant reminder that 'mine was bigger than yours . . . darling!'

More recently we were the guests of Chris and Christine Patrick in Sarasota, Florida. An hour south of the city is Charlotte Harbour where we fished for snook in the mangroves. Chris and I did quite well with fish of around six pounds. Gelly's best was 10lb! We then travelled on to Nashville, Tennessee, to stay with our good friend Peter Collins. We fished the J. Percy Priest Lake at dawn for hybrid striped bass. Peter and I had good fish to seven pounds but when my good lady decided she'd 'have a go', she landed, at 14lb, what our guide Jay Clementi described as a 'hog'!

Believe it or not, there are over twenty species that will take a fly in the rivers and lakes around Nashville, but our most interesting outing was for the buffalo carp. Our guide was Jim Mauries who runs Fly South, an excellent fly shop in town and highly recommended. He'd invited us to try for these strange fish on our last morning but asked if he could bring his son along. I imagined a lad of about twelve years old. Thomas turned out to be three and rode in a harness on Jim's back for the duration of the fishing. 'Buffalos' are tricky to catch. The fly must be presented about two feet in front of the fish as it 'grubs' along the bottom. When they take, it's an explosive experience and you'd better have enough backing on your reel. Jim and I caught some memorable fish and in case you are wondering why Gelly didn't catch the biggest one, the answer is simple. That was the morning she decided to have a lie in!

Rehearsing with 'the chaps', Granada Television, 1963.